ST/ESA/STAT/SER.F/85

Department of Economic and Social Affairs
Statistics Division

Studies in Methods   Series F, No. 85
Handbook of National Accounting

National Accounts:
A Practical Introduction

United Nations   New York, 2004

NOTE

Symbols of United Nations documents are composed of capital letters combined with figures.

The designations employed and the presentation of material in this publication do not imply the expression of any opinion whatsoever on the part of the Secretariat of the United Nations concerning the legal status of any country, territory, city or area or of its authorities, or concerning the delimitation of its frontiers or boundaries.

Where the designation "country or area" appears, it covers countries, territories or areas.

LIST OF ABBREVIATIONS

C.i.f.	Cost, insurance and freight
CPC	Central Product Classification (United Nations)
CPI	Consumer price index
FISIM	Financial intermediation services indirectly measured
F.o.b.	Free on board
GCF	Gross capital formation
GDP	Gross domestic product
GFCF	Gross fixed capital formation
GNDI	Gross national disposable income
GNI	Gross national income
IC	Intermediate consumption
ISIC	International Standard Industrial Classification of All Economic Activities
NCS	Net capital stock
NFC	Non-financial corporation
NPISHs	Non-profit institutions serving households
PIM	Perpetual inventory method
PPI	Producer price index

ST/ESA/STAT/SER.F/85

United Nations publication
Sales No. E.04.XVII.4
ISBN 92-1-161469-4

Preface

National Accounts: A Practical Introduction has been prepared as part of a series being developed by the member organizations of the Intersecretariat Working Group on National Accounts (ISWGNA) to assist countries in the implementation of the *System of National Accounts, 1993* (United Nations publication, Sales No.E.94.XVII.4). Its general objective is to provide an introduction to some basic concepts and structures of the System of National Accounts (SNA) to economists and policy makers who are not familiar with national accounts, as well as other newcomers to the field of national accounting. The text may serve as a guide to reading the SNA itself. In that sense, the text is written in as simple a style as possible, and therefore the detailed elaboration of concepts in both theory and practice is avoided. Simple exercises are included, whenever possible, to make concepts and structures clearer to readers. The handbook also provides an example of the complete system in Excel so that readers can trace the linkages in the system by looking at the formulas there. A compilation spreadsheet that can be used for compiling national accounts is also developed as part of the development of the handbook. It has been tested and used in many developing countries. Those supplements are posted on the web page of the United Nations Statistics Division as part of the series *Handbook of National Accounting*.

The text is not intended to replace either SNA or other handbooks. Compilers are expected to read the details in SNA as well as practical applications and methods presented in the handbooks prepared either by the United Nations Statistics Division, the Organisation for Economic Cooperation and Development (OECD), The International Monetary Fund (IMF) or the Food and Agriculture Organization of the United Nations (FAO). Many of those handbooks are posted on the web pages of the organizations that published them and can be obtained free of charge. The following handbooks have already been prepared or published:

- *Handbook on Non-profit Institutions in the System of National Accounts* (United Nations publication, Sales No. E. 03.XVII.9)
- *Use of the System of National Accounts in Economies in Transition* (United Nations publication, Sales No. E. 96.XVII.121)
- *Handbook of Input-Output Table Compilation and Analysis* (United Nations publication, Sales No. E.99.XVII.9)
- *Household Accounting: Experience in Concepts and Compilation* (United Nations publication, Sales No. E.00.XVII.16, vols.1 and 2)
- *Links between Business Accounting and National Accounting* (United Nations publication, Sales No.E.00.XVII.13)
- *A System Approach to National Accounts Compilation* (United Nations publication, Sales No.E.99.XVII.10)
- *Use of Macro Accounts in Policy Analysis* (United Nations publication, Sales, No. E.02.XVII.5)
- *Handbook on Non-Profit Institutions in the System of National Accounts* (United Nations publication, forthcoming)
- *Tourism Satellite Account: Recommended Methodological Framework* (United Nations publication, Sales No. E.01.XVII.9)
- *Balance of Payments Manual* (IMF, 1993)
- *Balance of Payments Compilation Guide* (IMF, 1994)
- *Government Finance Statistics Manual* (IMF, 2001)
- *A System of Economic Accounts for Food and Agriculture* (FAO, 1996)
- *Integrated Environmental and Economic Accounting* (United Nations publication, Sales No. E.93.XVII.12)

- *Handbook on Quarterly National Accounts*, (Statistical Office of the European Communities (Eurostat) 1999)
- *Quarterly National Accounts Statistics: Concepts, Data Sources and Compilation* (IMF, 2001)
- *Handbook on Measurement of the Non-Observed Economy* (OECD, 2002)
- *Measuring Capital: A Manual on the Measurement of Capital Stocks, Consumption of Fixed Capital and Capital Services* (OECD, 2001)
- *Handbook on Price and Volume Measures in National Accounts* (Eurostat, 2001)

The present handbook was prepared by Vu Quang Viet of the United Nations Statistics Division. Throughout the drafting of the handbook, valuable comments were provided by many experts in the field, particularly Cristina Hannig, Ivo Havinga, Karoly Kovacs, Mathias Reister and Mary Chamie of the United Nations Statistics Division, Brian Newson of Eurostat, Heidi Arboleda of the Economic and Social Commission for Asia and the Pacific, Estrella V. Dommingo of the National Statistical Coordinating Board of the Philippines and Yatimah bt. Sarjiman of the Department of Statistics of Malaysia. Ms. Arboleda provided a number of exercises for incorporation in the handbook.   Mathias Reister reviewed the draft carefully, providing important inputs to the rewriting of many chapters. The compilation worksheets were the result of the work over many years of Jan van Tongeren, Stefan Schweinfest and Vu Quang Viet, all of the United Nations Statistics Division.

The following are the web page addresses of various relevant international organizations and bodies:

- United Nations Statistics Division: http://unstats.un.org/unsd/
- International Monetary Fund: http://www.imf.org
- Organization for Economic Cooperation and Development: http://www.oecd.org/std
- World Bank: http://www.worldbank.org
- Food and Agriculture Organization of the United Nations: http://www.fao.org
- Statistical Office of the European Communities: http://europa.int/comm/eurostat/

CONTENTS

Part II: Integrated accounts by industries and institutional sectors

Part III: Data collection and estimation methods in SNA

Annex

Introduction

SNA AND ECONOMIC ANALYSIS

1. The System of National Accounts (SNA) helps economists to measure the level of economic development and the rate of economic growth, the change in consumption, saving, investment, debts and wealth (or net worth) for not only the total economy but also each of its institutional sectors (such as government, public and private corporations, households and non-profit institutions serving households);

2. With data from SNA, economists can either forecast the future growth of the economy or study impacts on the economy and its sectors of alternative government policies.

3. SNA promotes the integration of economic and related statistics in a system that is based on consistent economic and statistical concepts and methods. As such, it allows domestic and international comparative analysis.

SNA AS A SYSTEM

4. SNA consists of a coherent, consistent and integrated set of macroeconomic accounts, balance sheets and tables based on a set of internationally agreed concepts, definitions, classifications and accounting rules.

5. It provides a comprehensive and detailed record of the complex economic activities taking place within an economy and the interaction between different economic agents and groups of agents that takes place in markets or elsewhere.

PRESENTATION IN THREE PARTS

6. The present handbook covers:

   - The national economy as a whole vis-à-vis the rest of the world (part one)
   - Integrated accounts by industries and institutional sectors (part two)
   - Data collection and estimation methods in SNA (part three)

PART I

ACCOUNTS OF THE NATION

Chapter 1

Overview

A. INTRODUCTION

1.1.   National accounts is the macroeconomic depiction of the national income cycle using the double-entry bookkeeping principle of business accounting and a sequence of accounts to show the relationship between the various economic variables. The present chapter introduces the macroeconomic concepts and economic accounting identities underlying national accounts. In the section C, those concepts are presented in a numerical example that utilizes the accounting framework developed in national accounts. Section D gives a graphical presentation of the numerical example. Section E discusses some uses of indicators provided by national accounts and other economic statistics.

B. BASIC CONCEPTS AND VARIABLES OF NATIONAL ACCOUNTS

Supply and use

1.2.   For an economy, the total supply of goods and services must equal the total uses. Thus:

(1.1)   total supply of goods and services = total uses of goods and services

1.3.   In an open economy engaging in foreign trade, the total supply of goods and services consists of domestically produced output and imports. The uses consist of intermediate consumption, final consumption, gross capital formation and exports. Intermediate consumption consists of the goods and services consumed in the production process (excluding the consumption of fixed assets), while final consumption consists of the goods and services provided to the benefit of final consumers. Thus:

(1.2)   output + imports = intermediate consumption + final consumption + gross capital formation + exports

1.4.   A rearrangement of equation (1.2) allows for the identification of gross value added as output minus intermediate consumption. Leaving the issue of taxes and subsidies on goods and services aside, gross value added is the value of all goods and services produced during a production period but not immediately used up in the production process of that period. Hence, gross value added represents the value of all goods and services which are available for the different uses other than intermediate consumption. Thus:

(1.3)   gross value added = output – intermediate consumption

(1.4)   output – intermediate consumption = final consumption + gross capital formation + exports – imports

1.5.   The items intermediate consumption, final consumption and gross fixed capital formation on the uses (right) side of equation (1.2) are measured from the perspective of the consumer or purchaser. Their values take into account the taxes and subsidies on goods and services. While taxes on products increase, subsidies on products lower the prices payable by consumers. Yet output is measured from the perspective of producers in terms of the receipts receivable by them, leaving all of the taxes on goods and services aside while including subsidies on goods and services. Therefore, taxes on goods and services have to be added to output and subsidies subtracted from output in order to arrive at a uniform valuation of supply and uses.

(1.5)   output + taxes − subsidies − intermediate consumption = final consumption + gross capital formation + exports − imports

Gross domestic product

1.6.   On the left side of equation (1.5), we find the value of all goods and services produced in a period minus the goods and services consumed in the production process during that period, which is called gross domestic product (GDP). GDP can be measured by having the values for output and intermediate consumption aggregated across the various industries of an economy: GDP by production approach. Thus:

(1.6)   GDP = output + taxes − subsidies − intermediate consumption

1.7.   Output minus intermediate consumption can be replaced with gross value added.

(1.7)   GDP = gross value added + taxes − subsidies

1.8.   Looking at the right side of equation (1.5), gross domestic product can also be viewed as the value of all goods and services available for different domestic final uses or for exports: GDP by expenditure approach. Thus:

(1.8)   GDP = final consumption + gross capital formation + exports − imports

1.9.   The production process creates incomes for the owners of the inputs used in production but also for owners of capital and for the government. The value of those incomes is equal to gross domestic product. Hence, GDP can also be calculated as the sum of compensation of employees, taxes less subsidies and gross operating surplus/mixed income: GDP by income approach. Thus:

(1.9)   GDP = compensation of employees + taxes - subsidies + gross operating surplus / mixed income

1.10.   The components of gross operating surplus or mixed income and taxes less subsidies will be explained in more detail later. But it needs to be noted that the taxes less subsidies of equation (1.9) include not only all taxes less subsidies on products (i.e., goods and services) but also other taxes less subsidies on production.

Gross national income

1.11.   As an aggregate measure of production, gross domestic product refers to production of all resident units within the borders of a country, which is not exactly the same as the production of all productive activities of residents. Some of the productive activities of residents may take place abroad (for example temporary and seasonal labour working abroad). Conversely, some production taking place within a country may be attributed to temporary and seasonal foreign labour. The contribution of labour is accounted for through the compensation of employees paid to non-residents and received by the economy. In addition, some primary income generated within the country may go to non-resident units (for example, interest paid to providers of loans from abroad or dividends paid to non-resident owners of shares). Symmetrically, some primary incomes generated in the rest of the world may go to resident units. Thus, the concept of gross national income seeks to measure the net income due to their ownership of factors of production (labour, unproduced assets and capital) received by residents in a country. Residents are defined based on their centre of economic interest.

1.12. Hence, gross national income (GNI) is defined as follows:

(1.10) GNI = GDP + compensation of employees and property income from the rest of the world – compensation of employees and property income to the rest of the world

1.13. All GNI is not available for final uses domestically since some of it is transferred to other countries without anything being received in exchange, such as money sent to support dependants living in another country. Such transfers are called current transfers, and taking them into account leads to the following concept of gross national disposable income:

(1.11) gross national disposable income = GNI + current transfers from the rest of the world – current transfers to the rest of the world

1.14. Gross national disposable income is the income available for consumption and saving. Thus:

(1.12) gross national disposable income = final consumption expenditure + gross saving

Gross saving, gross capital formation and net lending

1.15. Gross saving is the difference between gross national disposable income and final consumption. Gross saving together with net capital transfers (capital transfers receivable less capital transfers payable) from the rest of the world provides the resources for investment in non-financial assets, which is called gross capital formation, i.e., for the net acquisition of fixed assets, such as residential and non-residential buildings, plants and equipments, and/or the increase in inventories. The difference between gross saving plus net capital transfers and gross capital formation is net borrowing or net lending from the rest of the world, depending whether uses exceed resources or vice versa: if it is negative it is net borrowing and if it is positive it is net lending. Thus:

(1.13) gross saving = gross national disposable income – final consumption

(1.14) net lending (+) / net borrowing (-) = gross saving + net capital transfers – gross capital formation

Net borrowing / net lending in financial accounts

1.16. Net borrowing / net lending is also reflected in transactions in financial assets and liabilities with the rest of the world. It is equal to the difference between net acquisition of financial assets and net incurrence of liabilities (foreign exchange, bonds, loans etc.). Thus:

(1.14) net lending (+) / net borrowing (-) = net acquisition of financial assets – net incurrence of liabilities

Changes in net worth

1.17. Net worth is the difference between the total value of non-financial and financial assets and the total value of liabilities of an economy. It is a measure of the net wealth of a nation. Change in net worth measures the change in wealth of a nation. It is equal to the difference between the change in the total value of assets and the change in the total value of liabilities. Besides the changes in net worth due to changes in prices that affect the valuation of assets and liabilities and natural incidents, such as discoveries or depletion of national resources and destruction due to natural calamities, the changes in net worth due to economic activities and transactions is the sum of gross saving and net capital transfers from abroad. The latter should also equal to gross capital formation less consumption of fixed capital and plus net lending (+)/net borrowing (-) from the rest of the world.

C. INTRODUCTION TO THE ACCOUNTING FRAMEWORK

Four basic accounting principles

1.18. The accounts are built on the basis of the following four simple accounting principles:

    a)   All transactions are recorded on an accrual basis (i.e., payable and receivable), not on a cash basis (i.e., received and paid);

    b)   Resources (receivables) are recorded on the right side and uses (payables) on the left side of the accounts. Liabilities are recorded on the right side and assets the left side of the accounts;

    c)   The balancing or closing item, which is always the last item on the uses side of the accounts, closes (balances) the account;

    d)   The balancing item is always the opening item of the next account, located as the first entry on the resources side of the account.

Sequence of accounts for the total economy

1.19. The sequence of accounts for the total economy begins with the production accounts and moves to the primary distribution of income account, the secondary distribution of income account, the use of income account, the capital account, the financial account and finally the balance sheet (see table 1.1).

1.20. The balance sheet provides information on the total fixed assets, total financial assets and total financial liabilities, classified by types of assets and liabilities of the economy at the beginning and end of the accounting period. The balance sheet is affected by three types of changes that occur during the course of the accounting period:

    a)   Changes in the balance sheet due to transactions;

    b)   Other changes in the volume of assets due to appearance and disappearance of assets;

    c)   Changes in balance sheets due to changes in prices.

1.21. Changes in the balance sheets due to transactions are the results of production activities and transactions with the rest of the world. Gross capital formation, after the consumption of fixed capital is deducted from it, adds to non-financial assets. Transactions in financial assets/liabilities change financial assets and liabilities. The difference in the total value of assets and total liabilities is change in net worth.

1.22. Other changes in the volume of assets are due to the appearance of resources, such as the discovery of sub-soil resources (oil or minerals, for example), or their disappearance due to depletion or natural calamities.

1.23.   Changes in balance sheets due to changes in prices include holding gains or losses   resulting from the revaluation of financial and non-financial assets.

1.24.   For the sake of simplicity, other changes in the volume of assets and changes in the balance sheets due to changes in prices are not included in the sequence of accounts provided in table T 1.1.

TABLE T1.1. SIMPLIFIED SEQUENCE OF ACCOUNTS OF THE DOMESTIC ECONOMY

		Uses	Resources
	Production account		
	Output of goods and services		100
Less	Intermediate consumption	40	
Equals	**Gross value added/GDP**	**60**	
	Primary distribution of income account		
	Gross value added/GDP		60
Plus	Compensation of employees and property income receivable from the rest of the world (ROW)		4
Less	Compensation of employees and property income payable to ROW	1	
Equals	**Gross national income**	**63**	
	Secondary distribution of income account		
	Gross national income		63
Plus	Current transfers receivable from ROW		1
Less	Less current transfers payable to ROW	2	
Equals	**Gross disposable income**	**62**	
	Use of income account		
	Gross disposable income		62
Less	Final consumption	40	
Equals	**Gross saving**	**22**	

		Uses	Resources
	Capital account		
	Gross saving		22
Less	Gross capital formation	15	
Plus	Capital transfers from ROW		1
Less	Capital transfers to ROW	1	
Equals	**Net lending to ROW**	**7**	

		Changes in assets	Changes in liabilities
	Financial account		
	Net acquisition of financial assets		
	Money	3	
	Loans	4	
Less	Net incurrence of liabilities		0
Equals	**Net lending to ROW**		**7**

		Assets	Liabilities
	Changes in the balance sheet due to transactions		
	Non-financial assets		
	Gross capital formation	15	
	Consumption of fixed capital	-1	
Less	Financial assets/financial liabilities	7	0
Equals	**Net worth**		**21**

Note: This simplified sequence of accounts eliminates other intermediate accounts, such as the generation of income account and the breakdown of primary income accounts into two separate accounts; it also does not present the balance sheets.

Account for the rest of the world

1.25.   The rest of the world (ROW) account is structured according to two principles:

a)   The transactions with the domestic economy are recorded from the perspective of the rest of the world;

b)   All transactions between the domestic economy and the rest of the world are recorded twice, as receivable in the accounts of the domestic economy and as payable in the rest of the world account or vice versa. For example, current transfers receivable from the rest of the world in the accounts for the domestic economy is recorded as current transfers payable to the rest of the world in the rest of the world account.

1.26.   Imports and exports are a special case. Thus:

a)   The item imports of the domestic economy in the rest of the world account is in fact the exports of the rest of the world and the item exports of the domestic economy are the imports of the rest of the world;

b)   The item imports in the rest of the world account represents the receivable created by the exports of goods and services from the rest of the world. Conversely, exports in the rest of the world account represents the payable created by the imports of the rest of the world.

1.27.   Since the rest of the world account is a counterpart of the domestic economy, the net lending (+) of the domestic economy is the net borrowing (-) of the rest of the world and vice versa.

TABLE T1.2. SIMPLIFIED ACCOUNT OF THE REST OF THE WORLD

		Uses	Resources
	Imports		10
Less	Exports	15	
Plus	Compensation of employees and property income receivable from ROW	4	
Less	Compensation of employees and property income payable to ROW		1
Plus	Current transfers receivable from ROW	1	
Less	Less current transfers payable to ROW		2
Plus	Capital transfers from ROW	1	
Less	Capital transfers to ROW		1
Equals	**Net borrowing of ROW**	**- 7**	
	Financial accounts	**Assets**	**Liabilities**
	Changes in financial assets	0	
Less	Changes in financial liabilities		7
	Money		3
	Loans		4
Equals	**Net borrowing of ROW**		**- 7**

Goods and services account

1.28.   The goods and services account has the following characteristics:

    a) It brings together the total supply and total uses of goods and services;
    b) It is balanced in itself and does not have a balancing item;
    c) Resources are recorded on the right side and uses on the left.

TABLE T1.3. GOODS AND SERVICES ACCOUNT

	Uses	Resources
Output of goods and services		100
Imports of goods and services		10
Intermediate consumption	40	
Final consumption	40	
Gross capital formation	15	
Exports of goods and services	15	
Total	110	110

D. GRAPHICAL PRESENTATION OF THE RELATIONSHIP OF BASIC CONCEPTS

1.29.   Equation (1.3) can be modified to obtain the value of output as the sum of gross value added and intermediate consumption. Thus:

    (1.15)   output = gross value added + intermediate consumption

1.30.   Equation (1.4) can be modified to obtain the value of output as the sum of intermediate and final uses. Thus:

    (1.16)   output = intermediate consumption + final consumption + gross capital formation + (exports – imports)

1.31.   Figure 1.1 shows the current transactions accounts of the domestic economy, the rest of the world account and the balance sheets in a schematic presentation. Net capital formation refers to gross capital formation less consumption of fixed capital. The so-called "net" transactions refer to receivable less payable; for example, net primary income equals primary income receivable less primary income payable. The relationship of total supply and total uses of goods and services and the balance sheets are shown horizontally. The current transactions of the domestic economy and the rest of the world account are shown vertically. For the purpose of clarity in the presentation, changes in the balance sheets are restricted to reflect only changes due to transactions and not volume and revaluation.

Figure F1.1: Sequence of accounts in a graphic presentation, with changes in the balance sheets reflecting economic transactions only

Opening balance sheet	Current transactions accounts of the domestic economy	Rest of the world account	Ending balance sheet

	Total supply of goods and services 110	=	Output 100					+	Imports 10	+10	

Current transactions accounts of the domestic economy:

- Total supply of goods and services 110 = Output 100 + Imports 10 → +10
-
- Total uses of goods and services 110 = Intermediate consumption 40 + Gross capital formation 15 + Final consumption 40 + Exports 15 → -15
- =
- Gross value added 60
- +
- Net primary income from rest of the world 3 → -3
- =
- GNI 63
- +
- Net current transfers from rest of the world -1 → +1
- =
- GNDI 62
- -
- Final consumption 40
- =
- Gross saving 22
- +
- Net capital transfers 0 → 0
- -
- Gross capital formation 15
- =
- Net lending 7 → -7

Opening balance sheet of non-financial assets 200	+	Net capital formation 15-1		=	Closing balance sheet of non-financial assets 214
Opening balance sheet of financial assets less liabilities 120	+	Financial assets less financial liabilities = net lending 7		=	Closing balance sheet of financial assets less liabilities 127
Opening balance sheet of the rest of the world [a] 100	+		Financial assets less financial liabilities = net borrowing -7	=	Closing balance sheet of the rest of the world[a] 93

[a]The International Monetary Fund calls net worth of the rest of the world "the international financial position"; positive value means that the economy has a negative position since the international financial position is shown from the perspective of the rest of the world.

11

E. USES OF NATIONAL ACCOUNTS INDICATORS

1.32.   National accounts time series provide most of the important data that are used in economic model building for the purposes of forecasting economic development, price analysis and estimating economic effects of government policies etc. The input-output table, which is derived from the supply and use tables in the system of national accounts, provides an important database for impact studies and productivity analysis at very detailed industrial and product levels. However, even without the support of sophisticated economic tools, indicators derived from aggregates in national accounts are already very useful for monitoring the overall performance of an economy, its strength as well as weakness. In some cases, those indicators need to be supplemented by other important indicators that are drawn from specialized statistics, such as monetary and government budget statistics. The discussion below does not pretend to be comprehensive but aims mainly to illustrate the importance of indicators that are derived from national accounts and specialized statistics in economic analysis.

Indicators based on national account aggregates

1.33.   Familiar indicators for monitoring the economy are real rate of growth in GDP, final consumption and gross capital formation (investment in fixed assets); saving rate (saving/GDP), investment rate (gross capital formation/GDP), government budget deficit / GDP, current external account balance / GDP, effective individual and corporate income tax rates etc. Those indicators can be derived directly from national accounts data. They not only show the performance of the economy over time but also allow comparison with other countries at the same level of development. Even without resorting to sophisticated modeling, the indicators derived from national accounts provide very useful information on the economy when evaluating them against stylized facts derived from the experiences in economic development studies. For example, in order to achieve a reasonable rate of growth, developing countries are expected to have an investment rate of at least 25 percent of GDP. A government budget deficit and a current external balance deficit over GDP of 3 percent and over would indicate trouble ahead if problems were not corrected. Another very useful aggregate in national accounts is change in inventories. The building up of inventories in relation to output in manufacturing industries is a signal for an economic slowdown and vice versa, assuming of course that change in inventories is not derived as a residual, as is the practice in some countries.

1.34.   Other indicators are derived by combining items in national accounts. For example, debt payment in relation to export (debt payment includes both interest payment and payment principal) is used as an indicator of debt payment capability, while export of manufacturing goods as a percentage of total exports is used as an indicator of export-led industrialization. A high ratio of government budget deficit over GDP and a large external account deficit would signal the need for policy adjustment. Large budget deficit may either crowd out private investment or generate higher inflation if the deficit is met with money printing instead of government borrowing. Of course, the analyst has to take many other factors into account. A high foreign debt service ratio coupled with a slowdown of exports would be a clear warning of a foreign debt payment crisis. Simple economic indicators provide a good tool for recognizing economic problems when the indicators cross some critical ratios.

Indicators based on specialized statistics

1.35.   National accounts are not the only source for economic indicators. Indicators from specialized statistics are equally important. Among money and banking statistics are a few ratios that are closely monitored. The rate of change in money supply[1] is used to monitor inflation prospects, while the non-

---

[1] Money supply can be derived from the financial accounts and the balance sheet, but it is cumbersome to do so, especially when money and banking statistics are used in compiling national accounts.

performing loan ratio and ratio of liability over asset are used as performance indicators of the banking system. The balance of payments, besides providing indicators that have been discussed above, also provides information on foreign exchange reserves and the current short-term liability denominated in foreign currencies. Those indicators are extremely important in detecting possible problems in the financial market.

1.36.   The financial crisis in East Asia and Association of South-East Asian Nations (ASEAN) countries in 1987 took place without warning since the performance ratios of the banking system and foreign exchange reserve were neither measured properly nor monitored closely. The economy seemed to be in good health before the impending crisis. Indicators on production, government budget and foreign trade balance looked favourable for almost all countries, except for the current external account deficits, which exceeded 6 percent of GDP. The shortfall, which was always expected to be met by capital inflow, turned out to be the reason for the devaluation of national currencies and deepening capital flight.

1.37.   Non-performing loan ratio is in general defined as loan non-payment beyond 3 months. In Asia, however, before 1997 loan non-payment over one year was not classified as non-performing. In addition, banks' liability over total asset is normally expected to be less than 1 in developed markets (meaning that net equity is zero), but in Asia the ratio of over 4 (meaning a great negative net equity) was commonly seen.

1.38.   Forward-binding contracts to sell foreign currencies (financial derivatives) were also not taken into account in liabilities denominated in foreign currencies in 1997 (see table T1.4 for the operational definition of foreign exchange reserves and total current liabilities denominated in foreign currencies.)

1.39.   General economic indicators are grouped into 11 groups and listed in table T1.4 for reference. The definition of the indicators and their possible uses are also indicated.

TABLE T1.4
ECONOMIC PERFFORMANCE INDICATORS

Indicators	Interpretation
Group 1. General economic level and performance	
▪ GDP per capita	▪ The level of economic development in comparison to other countries
▪ GDP rate of growth	▪ The performance of the economy
Group 2. Labour productivity and labour cost	
▪ Gross value added per worker per work hour (manufacturing)	▪ Labour productivity
▪ Compensation of employees per work hour	▪ Labour cost
Group 3. Income distribution	
▪ Compensation of employees / gross value added	▪ Income share of employees in GDP
▪ Operating surplus / gross value added	▪ Income share of capital in GDP
Group 4. Investment	
▪ Gross fixed capital formation / GDP	▪ Share of investment in capital goods in GDP
▪ Gross produced fixed assets / GDP	▪ Ratio used in estimating produced capital goods requirement for a given rate of growth in GDP.
▪ Gross fixed capital formation / change in GDP	▪ An approximation of capital/GDP ratio above (applicable only for the years with stable positive growth, commonly called ICOR)
▪ Gross fixed assets/ output by types of industries	▪ Capital – output ratios necessary for industry development planning
Group 5. Saving	
▪ Saving / GDP	▪ Saving rate of the nation
▪ Saving / gross fixed capital formation	▪ Domestic funding of investment
▪ Saving of an institutional sector / total saving	▪ Contribution of each sector to total saving
▪ Saving of households / disposable income of households	▪ Saving rate of households
Group 6. Performance of government	
▪ Government deficit / GDP	▪ Government deficit rate
▪ Revenue / expense (excluding payment on principal or incurrence of debt)	▪ If less than 1, government policy on budgeting needs to be seriously reviewed as recurrent revenue does not cover recurrent expense
▪ Fixed capital formation / total expenditure	▪ Share of investment in capital goods over total expenditure
▪ Interest payment / total expenditure	▪ Indicator of pressure of debt payment on government expenditure
▪ Taxes / GDP	▪ Government effort or tax burden
▪ Corporate taxes / corporate primary income balance	▪ Government effort or tax burden on corporations (right, fair, too high)
▪ Individual income taxes / gross national income of household	▪ Government factor on households (right, fair, too high)

Indicators	Interpretation
Group 7. Banking performance ■ Non-performing loan ratio (defined as loan non-payment beyond 3 months) ■ Liabilities / assets	■ Possibility of default ■ Banks' bill of health (to be healthy, the ratio is expected to be is lower than 1, which means that net equity is greater than zero)
Group 8. Foreign trade performance ■ Imports / GDP, import rate of growth ■ Exports / GDP, export rate of growth ■ (Exports + imports) / GDP ■ (Exports less imports) / GDP	■ Import reliance, growth factor ■ Export effort ■ Degree of openness of the economy ■ Export / import gap
Group 9. Balance of payment ■ Current external account deficit / GDP ■ (Exports less imports) / GDP ■ Debt payment (interest + principal) / export	■ Ability to service imports and current rate of economic growth (warning signal if over 3%) ■ Same as above ■ Ability to service foreign debt (expected to be lower than 30%)
Group 10. Foreign exchange reserve	■ Ability to finance imports and prevent foreign exchange crisis
Group 11. Prices ■ Producer price index, consumer price index, import price index and export price index ■ Interest rate ■ Foreign exchange rates ■ Stock exchange price index ■ Wage rate index	

15

Chapter 2

Production account and
goods and services account

A. OBJECTIVES

2.1.   The production account aims to measure output, intermediate consumption and ultimately the gross value added of every economic activity and every institutional sector in the economy. The sum of gross value added generated by different economic activities in the domestic economy is gross domestic product (GDP). GDP is the most important aggregate derived from the production account. GDP reflects the aggregate production of an economy. The growth rate in the volume of GDP summarizes the growth rate of the economy. Growth in GDP would allow for increases in either final consumption of the population and the government or investment in capital goods. The latter is expected to accelerate the growth rate of the economy.

2.2.   The present chapter covers the following topics:

a) Definition of gross value added;
b) Supply and uses of all goods and services in the economy: the balance of the supply and uses of goods and services describes the relationships of important aggregates in national accounts;
c) The production boundary of national accounts, i.e., what are the activities that are covered or not covered in national accounting;
d) The valuation principles in national accounts, i.e., how output and uses are valued;
e) The definition of the basic concepts in production accounting, such as output, intermediate consumption, final consumption, gross capital formation, exports and imports;
f) The measurement in practice of some important aggregates.

B. BASIC CONCEPTS AND RELATIONS OF GOODS AND SERVICES IN NATIONAL ACCOUNTS

1. GROSS DOMESTIC PRODUCT AND GROSS VALUE ADDED

2.3.   The System of National Accounts (SNA) defines GDP and gross value added operationally, i.e., how they are calculated. In the present section, GDP and value added are used interchangeably since they describe the same economic concept. Yet, as will be explained below, due to taxes and subsidies their valuation are not identical.

What do gross value added and gross domestic product measure?

2.4.   Gross value added and GDP measure the additional value of goods and services that are newly created in the economy and are available for domestic final uses or for exports.

2.5.   Output is the value of the goods and services which are produced by an establishment in the economy that become available for use outside that establishment. They are valued at market or equivalent market prices.

2.6.   Intermediate consumption is the cost of goods and services used in production.

2.7.   GDP is equal to the value of all goods and services produced in the economy (i.e., output) less the value of all goods and services used in the production processes (i.e., intermediate consumption). GDP is sometimes called in economic textbooks "output" or "net output". However, output has a different meaning in national accounts.

2.8.   Gross value added is calculated for every economic activity and then summed up to obtain the total gross value added for the whole economy. The total gross value added after some minor adjustment for taxes and subsidies is gross domestic product. Thus:

<u>Given</u>

Output	100	
Material costs	30	Intermediate
Service costs	10	consumption = 40

<u>Then</u>

	Output	100
<u>Less:</u>	Intermediate consumption	40
<u>Equals:</u>	Gross value added/GDP	60

2. SUPPLY AND USES OF GOODS AND SERVICES

2.9.   Gross value added can be more meaningfully interpreted within the context of supply and uses of goods and services in the economy. For the economy as a whole or for any product, the total supply must equal the total use.

2.10.   The total supply includes output and imports, while the total use includes final consumption, intermediate consumption, gross capital formation and exports. One may ask what happens to the goods that are not consumed? Those goods are in fact recorded as increase in inventories, which is a part of gross capital formation.

2.11.   Output is normally measured from the perspective of the producers, i.e., from the revenue received by them; that value, called output at basic prices, does not include product taxes that are collected on behalf of the government and includes subsidies provided by the latter. Thus, in order to balance the supply and use of goods and services paid by consumers at purchasers' prices, product taxes less subsidies must be added to the supply side (see table T2.1 and figure F2.1).

TABLE T2.1. SUPPLY AND USES OF GOODS AND SERVICES IN THE ECONOMY

Supply (resources) At purchasers' prices or equivalents		Uses At purchasers' prices or equivalents	
• Imports of goods f.o.b. and services	10	• Exports of goods f.o.b. and services	15
• Output at basic prices	95	• Intermediate consumption at purchasers' prices	40
• Taxes less subsidies on products	5	• Gross capital formation at purchasers' prices	15
		• Final consumption at purchasers' prices	40

FIGURE F2.1. SUPPLY AND USES OF GOODS AND SERVICES

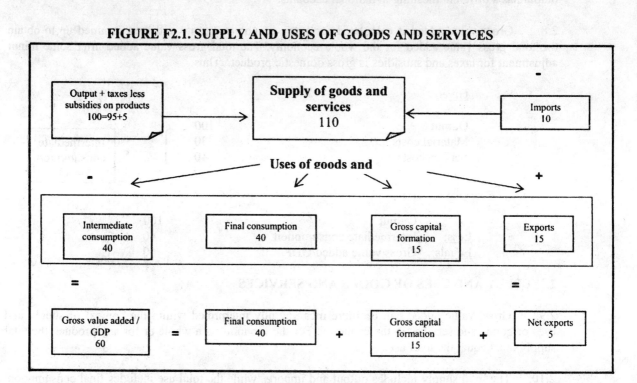

3. BASIC RELATIONSHIPS IN NATIONAL ACCOUNTS

2.12.   The manipulation of the equality of the total supply and the total use allows for the derivation of the following basic relationships in the total economy:

(2.1)   (output   + taxes less subsides on products) + import = intermediate consumption + gross capital formation + final consumption + exports

Or:

(2.2)   (output - intermediate consumption) + taxes less subsidies on products = gross capital formation + final consumption + (exports - imports)

By definition:

(2.3)   gross value added = output – intermediate consumption

Then:

(2.4)   Gross value added + taxes less subsidies on products   = gross capital formation + final consumption + (exports - imports)

By definition:

(2.6)   gross domestic product (GDP) = gross value added + taxes less subsidies on products

Then:

(2.7)   GDP = gross capital formation + final consumption + exports – imports

GDP is an output concept

2.13.   Equation (2.7) above, when reorganized as set out below, would allow for an interesting interpretation of output. It shows the uses of GDP as "final uses", consisting of domestic uses and exports. Thus, GDP is clearly a concept based on output and its uses and is not an income concept.

(2.8)   GDP = (final consumption + gross capital formation – imports) + exports
(2.9)   GDP = domestic final uses + exports

4. OVERALL APPROACHES TO CALCULATING GDP

2.14.   **Production approach**: GDP can be calculated by adding taxes less subsidies on products to the total value added, which is derived by subtracting intermediate consumption from output in equation (2.3).

2.15.   **Final expenditure approach**: GDP can also be obtained by adding final uses (domestic plus the rest of the world) together.

2.16.   **Income approach**: GDP can also be obtained by adding together the income components that make up value added (value added is elaborated below). GDP by income approach covers only the incomes generated within the domestic economy.

5. COMPONENTS OF VALUE ADDED

2.17.   In principle, GDP can be computed by adding together the components of value added and taxes less subsidies on products.

2.18.   Value added includes:

   a) **Compensation of employees:** Compensation of employees is the total remuneration in cash or in kind payable by employers to employees for the work done. Direct social transfers from employers to their employees or retired employees and their family, such as payments for sickness, educational grants and pensions that do not set up an independent fund, are also imputed to compensation of employees;

b) **Other taxes less subsidies on production:** Other taxes less subsidies on production are taxes payable by employers to carry out production, irrespective of sales or profitability. They may be payable as license fees or as taxes on the ownership or use of land, buildings or other assets used in production or on the labour employed or on the compensation of employees paid. They are not taxes paid on values of sales or produced outputs, which are called taxes on products;

c) **Consumption of fixed capital:** Consumption of fixed capital is the cost of fixed assets used up in production in the accounting period;

d) **Gross operating surplus**: Gross operating surplus is the residual obtained by deducting the above components from value added. Thus, gross operating surplus includes interest payable to lenders of financial assets, or rent payable to rentiers of non-produced assets, such as land, sub-soil assets or patents.

2.19.   Gross operating surplus of corporate enterprises can also be estimated by summing over:

a) Additions to retained earnings;
b) Depreciation and depletion;
c) Bad debt allowance;
d) Property income payable;
e) (-) Property income receivable;
f) Current transfers payable;
g) (-) Current transfers receivable;
h) (-) Gains (net of loss) on sales on fixed assets and securities.

2.20.   In practice, value added from corporations may be obtained by the income approach, but value added from unincorporated activities when no formal accounts are available must be obtained by the production approach.

2.21.   Explanations of the above concepts may be obtained by consulting the handbook *Links between Business Accounting and National Accounting* (United Nations publication, Sales No. E.00.XVII.13)

C. PRODUCTION BOUNDARY AND PRINCIPLES OF VALUATION

1. PRODUCTION BOUNDARY

2.22.   Not all economic activities are treated as economic activities and included in the production boundary of the System of National Accounts. Except for the services of owner-occupied housing and paid domestic staff, all personal and domestic services that are produced and consumed within the same households, such as cleaning, decoration, cooking, caring for and educating children, caring for sick and old people, maintenance and repair of dwellings and durables, transportation of household members etc. are excluded.

2.23.   Included in the production boundary of SNA are:

a) The production of all individual or collective goods and services that are supplied or intended to be supplied to production units other than themselves;
b) The own-account production of all goods that are retained by their producers for their own final consumption or gross capital formation;

c) The own-account production of housing services by owner-occupiers and personal services produced by the employment of paid domestic staff;

d) The production of all agricultural goods for sale or own final use and their subsequent storage; the gathering of uncultivated crops; forestry; wood-cutting; the collection of firewood; hunting and fishing; carrying of water; the processing (threshing, milling, preserving etc.) of agricultural and other food products; the weaving of cloth, dress-making and tailoring, the production of footwear, pottery, utensils, furnishings etc.

2.24. Also included in the production boundary are illegal and hidden goods and services:

a) Production and distribution of goods and services whose sale, distribution or possession is forbidden by law, such as narcotics, smuggling of goods and prostitution;

b) Production of goods and services which are deliberately concealed from public authorities in order to avoid the payment of taxes, the meeting of legal standards or compliance with administrative procedures.

2.25. The SNA production boundary has been extended to include natural growth of cultivated forests, the development of entertainment, literary or artistic originals and the leasing of the right to exploit those assets. Also included is the development of software on own account that can be used for more than one year.

2. VALUATION OF GOODS AND SERVICES IN SNA

2.26. Outputs, whether or not sold, are valued at market or equivalent market prices. Market prices are the actual and economically significant prices agreed upon by the transactors. SNA does not set a standard for economically significant price, but most countries decide that it must cover at least half of production costs. There are three types of market prices of the same good due to taxes and subsidies. The reason for different kinds of prices is that what the purchaser pays and the seller receives is not identical (see figure F2.2 for their relationships):

a) **Basic price** is the amount received by the producer from the purchasers for a unit of output. Thus, it should exclude any tax assessed on the output (i.e., taxes on products) and include any subsidies on the output that the producer receives. It also excludes any transport charges invoiced separately by the producer. The measurement of output at basic prices makes value reflect better volume;

b) **Producer price** is the basic price plus taxes on the output invoiced to the purchaser less subsidies received by the producer from the government;

c) **Purchasers' price** is the amount paid by the buyer for a unit of output less any taxes invoiced by the seller but deductible by the purchaser. It should be equal to the producer price plus transport costs and trade margins on products, which are not separately invoiced.[2]

2.27 **Output at production costs**. Output is recommended to be measured at production costs when products have no market price. Output at production costs is the sum of the following items:

a) Intermediate consumption;

b) Compensation of employees;

---

[2] Separately invoiced transport costs are treated as a separate purchase of transport service.

c) Consumption of fixed capital (which is the cost of produced fixed assets used in providing services);

d) Other taxes on production.

2.28. Figure F2.2 shows the relationship between basic price, producer price and purchasers' price of a product in the market when it moves from the producer to the consumer at the end of the circulation process, either directly or through wholesale and retail channels. The basic price is the value of a product unit received by the producer, including subsidies on the product, but excluding the taxes paid on the product to be transferred to the government. The producer price is the price the producer charges at the time when it leaves the production unit (which includes taxes but less subsidies on the product). The purchasers' price may go through many stages of circulation; each stage may incur taxes, subsidies, transport and trade margins. At each stage, a product has a different purchaser price from the point of view of the purchasers. Figure F2.3 illustrates the circulation of products from the producer to the consumer and the taxes and costs involved.

FIGURE F2.2. RELATIONSHIPS BETWEEN BASIC, PRODUCER AND PURCHASERS' PRICES

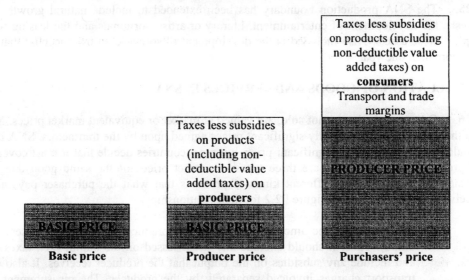

FIGURE F2.3. PROCESS OF GOODS CIRCULATION ON THE MARKET

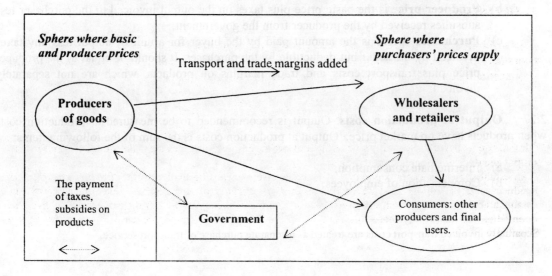

22

3. VALUATION OF NATIONAL ACCOUNTS AGGREGATES

2.29.   Goods and services may be valued differently, but the valuation should satisfy three principles:

    a) Uniformity in the elements when they have to be aggregated;
    b) Avoidance of double counting;
    c) Purchasers' price = basic price + trade margins + taxes less subsidies on products.

2.30.   In the equality of supply and uses of goods and services (see equation (2.1)), the total supply and the total uses are in purchasers' prices and each aggregate is in purchasers' prices or equivalents. The category "output + taxes less subsidies on products" is in fact output in purchasers' prices, although the element "output" is in basic prices. "Output" in basic prices already includes the output of trade services, so that trade margins need not be included again in order to avoid double counting. However, taxes less subsidies on products must be added to obtain output in purchasers' prices.

2.31.   To conform with valuation principles, when output is measured at **basic prices** equations (2.3) and (2.6) can be specified more clearly as follows:

    (2.10) gross value added at basic prices = output at basic prices – intermediate consumption at purchasers' prices

    (2.11) GDP = gross value added at basic prices + taxes less subsidies on products

2.32.   To conform with valuation principles, when output is measured at producer prices equations (2.3) and (2.6) can be specified as follows:

    (2.12) gross value added at producer prices = output at producer prices – intermediate consumption at purchasers' prices

    (2.13) GDP = gross value added at producer prices + import duties[3]

D. BASIC DEFINITIONS OF OTHER AGGREGATES OF GOODS AND SERVICES IN NATIONAL ACCOUNTS

1. DEFINITION OF OUTPUT

2.33.   Output is the value of the goods and services which are produced by an establishment in the economy that become available for use outside that establishment[4] (see table T.2.2, for type of producer and output in terms of market, non-market and for own final use).

---

[3] Import duties have to be added since output at producer prices includes taxes on products only for domestic output and does not include import duties.

[4] An establishment is a production unit of an enterprise, which is normally identified by the kind of product it produces and the ability to account for its cost of production. An enterprise may have more than one establishment. Products which are produced for intermediate consumption in the same establishment are not counted as products. Only those that are supplied to another establishment (even of the same enterprise) are counted as products.

2.34.   Losses or wastage in production and distribution will not be counted as output. For example, electricity produced and lost in distribution is not part of output.

2.35.   The output of goods and services is normally recorded when their production is completed. However, if it takes more than one accounting period to produce a unit of output, then work-in-progress must be recorded at the end of the accounting period.

2.36.   Output of trade services is the margin realized from a good purchased for resale. It is equal to sale less the cost to repurchase the good sold at the time it is sold.

2.37.   Output of a bank is its implicit and explicit service charges, which are only a small part of interest charges (see detailed definition in paras. 2.79-2.87 below)

2.38.   Output of insurance or pension funds is the service charge, which is a small part of premiums or contributions paid (see detailed definition in paras. 2.79-2.87 below)

2.39.   Non-market output, which is provided free or sold at economically insignificant prices, is measured at production costs (see paras. 2.29-2.32 above for a definition of how non-market output is valued). Non-market output includes those of the following:

    a)   General government;
    b)   Non-profit institutions serving households;
    c)   Own-account construction (own account production means production for own use);
    d)   Own-account research and development;
    e)   Own-account software development.

TABLE T2.2. TYPES OF PRODUCERS AND OUTPUT

		Market producers	Producers for own final use	Other non-market producers
		Include establishments in: ▪ Large corporations and ▪ Small unincorporated enterprises (may be owned by households) most of whose products is marketed	Household unincorporated enterprises, which includes: ▪ Subsistence farmers etc. ▪ Households engaged in the construction of their own dwellings and other goods for own consumption)	Include: ▪ General government ▪ Non-profit institutions serving households
Type of output produced	Market output	Mostly	Some (e.g., grains, vegetables, etc.)	Some (e.g., fees paid for government services, sales of government's publications)
	Output for own final use	Some, e.g.: ▪ Own-account capital formation ▪ Own-account software development ▪ Research and development ▪ Output retained for final consumption by owners of unincorporated enterprises	Mostly (e.g., produce of subsistence farmers)	Some (e.g., government's own capital formation)
	Other non-market output	None	None	Mostly (e.g., free services provided by government and non-profit institutions serving households)

2. DEFINITION OF INTERMEDIATE CONSUMPTION

2.40. Intermediate consumption includes goods and services which are entirely used up by producers in the course of production to produce output of goods and services during the accounting period.

2.41. Durable goods which may be classified as capital goods since they are used as the tools of production over a number of years (saws, spades, knives, axes, hammers and screwdrivers etc.) may be included in intermediate consumption if their prices are below a certain low value. The criterion is normally decided by statistical office or tax authority, depending on the stage of economic development of the country.

2.42. Intermediate consumption excludes other production costs, such as labour cost, financial costs and production taxes.

2.43. The labour and financial costs and production taxes are costs to business firms but are treated in SNA as incomes generated for the economy in the production process.

3. DEFINITION OF FINAL CONSUMPTION

2.44. Final consumption includes goods and services which are used by households or the community to satisfy their individual wants and social needs. Thus, final consumption is broken down into:

   a) Final consumption expenditure of households;
   b) Final consumption expenditure of general government;
   c) Final consumption expenditure of non-profit institutions serving households.

2.45. For households, all consumed goods, whether durable (cars, refrigerators, air-conditioners etc.) or non-durable (food, clothes), are part of final consumption, with the exception of purchases, own-construction or improvements of residential housing, which are treated as part of gross capital formation.

2.46. Included in final consumption expenditure of households are:

   a) All goods and services bought for final consumption by households;
   b) All goods produced for own final consumption by households, including those goods and
   c) services produced by household enterprises and retained for final consumption; Domestic services produced for own final consumption by employing paid staff, such as servants, cooks, gardeners and chauffeurs;
   d) Services of owner-occupied dwellings (whose imputed values are equivalent market rentals);
   e) All goods and services acquired by households in barter transactions for final consumption;
   f) All goods and services received by households as payment in kind from producers;
   g) Expenditures incurred in "do-it-yourself" decoration, maintenance and routine repairs of own dwellings and personal goods;
   h) Payment to government units to obtain various kinds of licenses, permits, certificates, passports etc.

i) Explicit and imputed service charges on household uses of financial intermediation services provided by banks, insurance companies, pension funds etc.

2.47. Included in the final consumption expenditure of general government and non-profit institutions serving households are:

a) Non-market output other than own-account capital formation, which is measured by production costs less incidental sales of government output;

b) Expenditure on market goods and services that are supplied without transformation and free of charge to households (referred to by SNA as social transfers in kind).

4. DEFINITION OF EXPORTS AND IMPORTS OF GOODS AND SERVICES

2.48. Exports and imports between the domestic economy and the rest of the world are transactions between residents and non-residents of an economic territory (see figure F2.4).

2.49. A transaction of goods and services (sales, barter, gifts) from residents to non-residents is an export and from non-residents to residents is an import. A transfer of income of the same value must also be imputed.

2.50. Exports and imports exclude all transactions in land, buildings and non-movable non-produced assets, and in financial assets (stocks, bonds, money, monetary gold etc.) SNA takes an exception rule on land, buildings and non-movable non-produced assets since they are still used for production purposes in the domestic economy. Financial assets are neither goods nor services.

2.51. Exports and imports occur when there are changes of ownership between residents and non-residents, regardless of whether there are corresponding physical movements of goods across borders. However, there are three exceptions that require imputation of changes of ownership: (a) financial leasing, (b) deliveries between affiliated enterprises and (c) goods sent for significant processing to order or repairs. Goods bought from non-residents and sold to non-residents by commodity dealers within the same accounting period are not recorded as exports or imports.

Residents and non-residents

2.52. An institutional unit, (a household, an enterprise, a non-profit unit etc.) is a resident unit when it has a centre of economic interest in the economic territory in question. To have a centre of economic interest in a territory is to have ownership of land or ownership of structures or to engage in production in a territory for a long period of time (at least one year).

2.53. Military personnel and civil servants, including diplomats employed abroad by an economic territory, are residents of the territory that employs them.

2.54. Students are residents of their country of origin, however long they study abroad.

2.55. International organizations are not considered residents of any national economy, but their workers are residents of the economy in which they are expected to have their abode for at least one year.

2.56.   Owners of buildings and non-produced assets, such as land, sub-soil assets or legal constructs (leases etc.), even if they are not actually residents, are treated as residents of the economy since such assets remain in the economy and serve the production activities of the economy. Transactions involving them are not part of exports and imports.

FIGURE F2.4. EXPORTS AND IMPORTS AS TRANSACTIONS BETWEEN RESIDENTS AND NON-RESIDENTS

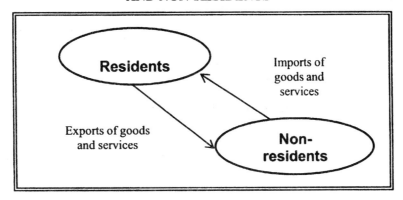

Valuation of exports and imports

2.57.   Exports are valued free on board (f.o.b.) i.e., at the prices at the domestic customs frontier before being shipped out. They should by definition be equivalent to purchasers' prices since they include domestic transport and trade costs to bring the good to the ports, and also include taxes less subsidies on products paid by the purchasers or received by the producers.

2.58.   Imports must also be valued f.o.b. but are valued at the prices at the foreign custom frontier.

2.59.   Imports are normally valued cost, insurance, freight (c.i.f.), at the domestic custom frontier by customs. To derive imports f.o.b., cost of freight and insurance services between the two borders must be estimated and deducted from imports c.i.f. Freight and insurance services on imports may be provided by either residents or non-residents. Those provided by non-residents are imports but those provided by residents are domestic output. Imports f.o.b. avoid counting domestic output as imports and avoid double counting imported freight and insurance services since they are already included in data on imports of services.

5. DEFINITION OF GROSS CAPITAL FORMATION

2.60.   Gross capital formation in SNA is the same as the concept of *investment in capital goods* used by economists. It includes only produced capital goods (machinery, buildings, roads, artistic originals etc.) and improvements to non-produced assets. Gross capital formation measures the additions to the capital stock of buildings, equipment and inventories, i.e., the additions to the capacity to produce more goods and income in the future.

2.61.   Non-produced assets, such as land, natural resources and patented entities, may also be used as capital in an establishment or enterprise or the whole economy but are not part of the gross capital formation in SNA.

2.62.   In business accounting, investment in capital goods may include acquisitions less disposals of non-produced assets (land, mineral resources etc.). At the national level, the inclusion or exclusion of non-produced assets would not affect the value of investment in capital goods since the sale of a non-produced asset by one economic entity will be offset by a purchase of the same asset by another economic entity.

Common usage of the term "investment"

2.63.   In common usage (business and households), the concept of investment is very broad. It includes:

a) Investment in produced and non-produced assets (i.e., patents, goodwill, natural resources);
b) Investment in financial assets.

Components of gross capital formation

2.64.   Gross capital formation, which is a major factor in changing the values of non-financial assets in the economy, includes (see table T2.3 for the classification of assets and the effects of gross capital formation on assets):

a) Gross fixed capital formation;
b) Changes in inventories;
c) Acquisition less disposals of valuables (such as jewelry and works of art).

Gross fixed capital formation

2.65.   Gross fixed capital formation includes:

a) Acquisition less disposal of new or existing produced assets, such as dwellings, other building structures, machinery and equipment, cultivated assets (e.g., trees and livestock), mineral exploration, computer software, entertainment, literary or artistic originals, and other intangible fixed assets;
b) Costs of ownership transfers on non-produced, non-financial assets, such as land and patented assets;
c) Major improvements to produced and non-produced, non-financial assets that extend the lives of assets (e.g. reclamation of land from sea, clearance of forests, rock etc., draining of marches or irrigation of forests, and prevention of flooding or erosion);
d) Acquisition can be in terms of purchase, own-account production, barter, capital transfer in kind, financial leasing, natural growth of cultivated assets and major repairs of produced assets;
e) Disposal can be in terms of sale, barter, capital transfer in kind or financial lease. Exceptional losses, such as those due to natural disasters (fire, drought etc.) are not recorded as disposal.

Changes in inventories

2.66.   Inventories include:

a) Materials and supplies;
b) Work-in-progress (growing crops, maturing trees and livestock, uncompleted structures, uncompleted other fixed assets, partially completed film productions and software);
c) Finished goods;

d) Goods for resale.

TABLE T2.3. CLASSIFICATION AND FORMATION OF NON-FINANCIAL ASSETS

Types of non-financial assets	Opening balance sheet	Changes in the balance sheets			Other changes in balance sheet	Closing balance sheet
		Gross capital formation		Consumption of fixed capital		
		Acquisition less disposal, cost of major improvements	Cost of ownership transfers			
	(1)	(2)	(3)	(4)	(5)	(1)+(2)+(3) -(4)+ (5)
Produced assets						
Produced fixed assets						
Tangible fixed assets						
Dwellings						
Other buildings and structures						
Non-residential buildings						
Other structures						
Machinery and equipment						
Transport equipment						
Other machinery and equipment						
Cultivated assets						
Livestock for breeding, dairy, etc.						
Vineyards, orchards and other plantations						
Intangible fixed assets						
Mineral exploration						
Computer software						
Entertainment, literary or artistic originals						
Other non-tangible fixed assets						
Inventories						
Materials and supplies						
Work in progress						
Finished goods						
Goods for resale						
Valuables						
Non-produced assets		Not applicable		Not applicable		
Tangible non-produced assets						
Land						
Subsoil assets						
Coal, oil and natural gas reserves						
Metallic mineral reserves						
Non-metallic mineral reserves						
Non-cultivated biological resources						
Water resources						
Intangible non-produced assets						
Patented entities						
Leases and other transferable contracts						
Purchased goodwill						
Other intangible non-produced assets						

E. MEASUREMENT ISSUES

1. ESTIMATION OF MARKET OUTPUT FROM SALES

2.67.   Output is valued as the product of the quantity of output and the price of one unit of the product at basic prices (excluding all product taxes and trade and transport costs to deliver the goods from producers to buyers). This method is applied to many crops or livestock.

2.68.   However, quantity output normally cannot be directly obtained by asking producers, particularly in manufacturing and service industries, since they are only familiar with sales and cost of sales, which are recorded in their business accounts and normally called financial statements.

2.69.   Output at basic prices is, in theory, computed as follows:

    a) Output = sales less sale taxes plus subsidies + change in inventory of finished and semi-finished goods;

    b) Change in inventory = closing inventory - opening inventory;

    c) Addition to inventory must be valued at the market prices at the time goods entered inventory;

    d) Withdrawal from inventory must be valued at the market prices at the time goods are withdrawn.

TABLE T2.4. ESTIMATION OF OUTPUT FROM SALES: AN EXAMPLE

	Calculating operations	T_0	T_1	T_2	T_3
Information given					
1. Sales net of taxes and plus subsidies			80	120	272
2. Price index			100	125	200
3. Value of inventory at end of period (book value)		0	40	30	16
4. Change in inventory (book value)	$= (T_i - T_{i-1})$ applied to line (3)		40	-10	-14
Derived data					
5. Value of inventory at constant prices	= Line (3)*100/ line (2)	0	40	24	8
6. Change in inventory at constant prices	$= (T_i - T_{i-1})$ from line (5)		40	-16	-16
7. Change in inventory at current prices	= Line (6) * line (2)/100		40	-20	-32
8. Output at basic price	= Line (1) + line (7)		120	100	240

In the example, the estimation method provides an exact value of output, which is possible because the stock of physical inventory is assumed taken at the end of each period and revalued at the same time (line 3). In general, inventories are valued differently in business, accounting either by LIFO, FIFO or as above. Therefore, this Canadian method is only an approximation. See *Links between Business Accounting and National Accounting*, (United Nations publication, Sales No. E.00.XVII.13), chap. III.

2.70.   The following approximate formula can be used to estimate change in inventory at current prices for computing output (see example in table T2.4):

    a) Deflate ending inventory by its appropriate price index;

    b) Calculate change in inventory at the base year price;

    c) Calculate change in inventory in current price by inflating the inventory at the base year price with the same price index.

2. CROP OUTPUT

2.71.   The output of a crop is simply the product of the quantity of output and the unit price at basic prices when the growing and harvesting of crops occur during the same accounting period.

2.72.   The output of a crop (or natural growth of cultivated assets) may be generated for the entire time span covering more than one accounting period from the time the crop is sown to the time it is harvested. To obtain the output for every accounting period, the harvested products less losses and wastes (i.e., finished products) must be allocated to each period on the basis of the share of actual costs (i.e., materials, services and labour) incurred during the period. Assuming that the costs incurred equally each month during the crop season and the total value of finished products is 100 for the case shown in table T2.5, the first year will be allocated 4/11 and the second year 7/11 of the finished products. The example assumes that prices do not change; otherwise, work-in-progress has to be revalued to current market prices.

2.73.   The output of the first year is treated as work-in-progress to be entered into inventory (a part of gross capital formation). That inventory will have to be withdrawn after the crop is harvested the following year (negative change in inventory in gross capital formation). This example assumes there is no change in price.

2.74. The principle described above is not yet widely practiced. Most countries assign output and its associated costs to the time when crop is harvested. This latter practice is particularly common in the compilation of quarterly accounts.

TABLE T2.5. ESTIMATION OF CROP OUTPUT: AN EXAMPLE

First accounting year				Second accounting year										
Crop sown										Crop harvested				
-4	-3	-2	-1	1	2	3	4	5	6	7	8	9	10	11
Output (last 4 months) = 36.4 Change in inventory = 36.4				Output (first 7 months) = 63.6 Change in inventory = -36.4										

3. LIVESTOCK OUTPUT

2.75.   The formula for estimating the output of livestock in general is based on the following relationship:

> Output of live animals + imports = animals slaughtered or died of natural causes + exports + change in animal stock

2.76.   Animals have to be divided into two major types:

a) Those that are treated as fixed assets; such as adult dairy animals, animals raised for their wool, breeding animals or draught animals more than one year old;

b) Those that are treated as work-in-progress, such as those reared for slaughter or young animals (one year old and less) reared to be used as fixed assets;

c) Output can be first estimated in terms of number and weight and then valued at basic prices.

2.77.   For more detail, see 1993 SNA, paras. 6.94-6.100; and Food and Agriculture Organization of the United Nations, *A System of Economic Accounts for Food and Agriculture* (Rome, 1996).

4. OUTPUT OF WHOLESALE AND RETAIL SERVICES

2.78.   Output of wholesale and retail services, which is called trade margin, is the difference between sale less the cost to repurchase the good sold at the time it is sold (see table T2.6).

TABLE T2.6. OUTPUT OF WHOLESALE AND RETAIL SERVICES: AN EXAMPLE

T-3	T-2	T-1	T
• Product A was bought at 100			• Product A was sold at 120 • Market value if the product sold is to be restocked: 110

In theory: output at basic price = trade margin = 120 – 110 = 10; output is at basic price since sale is normally recorded net of taxes on products invoiced to purchasers.
In practice: trade margin = 120 – 100 = 20 if inventories are not properly valued (see paras. 2.67-2.70 above on estimation of market output from sales; the difference of 10 is called holding gain, which is not part of output.

5. OUTPUT OF FINANCIAL INTERMEDIATION SERVICES

2.79.   Output of financial intermediation companies in banking, insurance services and pension fund services cannot be directly measured since such companies do not normally charge their customers for their services except for some minor incidental services. Banks earn their main source of income by the difference between the interest earned by providing loans and the interest paid on deposits. Pension funds and insurance companies accept contributions and invest them in order to pay their customers. Their output has to be measured indirectly.

Output of banking services

2.80.   Output of banking services is measured as follows:

output = explicit service charges + implicit service charges
= explicit service charges + property income receivable (excluding those receivable on own funds) – interest payments.

2.81.   The output of central bank may be calculated by production costs if the output calculated by the above formula fluctuates unreasonably as a result of its monetary policy.

Output of insurance services

2.82.   Output of insurance services is measured as follows:

Output =		total actual premiums earned (excluding prepayments of premiums)
	plus	total premium supplements (equal to the income gained from the investment of the insurance technical reserves, which also include prepayments, reserves for pending and unexpected claims)
	minus	total claims due (including outstanding claims that are not yet paid)
	plus	change in the actuarial reserves and reserves for with-profits insurance

2.83.   The output of insurance services is very likely to fluctuate widely over the years due to the movement of claim payment. Some countries have introduced the five-year moving average, taking the average of the current year and the preceding four years to reduce the up-and-down of output and thus value added. When claims are too high, particularly when catastrophic accidents happen, output may become negative and claims may have to be spread to future years in the calculation of output and value added. The international organizations are studying the issues in order to come up with a more appropriate solution. However, one possibility is to measure output of only catastrophic accidents by production costs.

Output of pension fund services

2.84.   Output of pension fund services is measured as follows:

output =		total actual pension contributions
	plus	total supplementary contributions (equal to the income from the investment of the pension funds technical reserves
	minus	benefits due
	plus	change in the actuarial reserves

Output of other financial services

2.85.   Output of foreign exchange and securities dealers is measured by trade margins (the difference between the purchasers' price of the dealer less the purchasers' price for the buyer), but holding gains due to price fluctuation must be excluded (see output of wholesale and retail trade services).

2.86.   Output of other financial intermediation services, such as security, loan and insurance brokers and advisers on investment, is measured by fees or commissions charged to customers.

2.87.   Moneylenders who lend their own funds do not generate output since they do not engage in financial intermediation.

6. ESTIMATION OF INTERMEDIATE CONSUMPTION FROM PURCHASE OF MATERIALS

2.88.   The use of goods in production, which is part of intermediate consumption, cannot be obtained directly by asking producers. Business accounts kept by the producers record only purchases of materials and inventories of materials. The uses of goods in production can be obtained by the following formula:

uses of materials = purchases of materials - change in inventory of materials

2.88.   For approximating change in inventory, the method used for output should be applied.

2.90. For a detailed discussion of the treatment of inventories in SNA see *Handbook of Input-Output Table Compilation and Analysis* (United Nations publications, Sales No. E.99.XVII.9) chap. V, appendix A.

7. ESTIMATION OF OUTPUT BY PRODUCTION COSTS

2.91.   Output measured by production costs is the sum of the following costs:

a)   Intermediate consumption;
b)   Compensation of employees:
   i)   Wages and salaries in cash and in kind;
   ii)   Employers' social contribution to social security, insurance schemes and pension funds;
   iii) Benefits for sickness, unemployment, retirement etc. paid by employers directly to employees (which are called imputed social contributions);
c)   Consumption of fixed capital;
d)   Other taxes, less subsidies, on production.

8. ESTIMATION OF CONSUMPTION OF FIXED CAPITAL

2.92.   Consumption of fixed capital is a cost of production. It measures the decline in the current values of the stock of fixed assets owned and used by producers as a result of physical deterioration, normal obsolescence and normal accidental damages during the accounting period.

2.93.   Thus, consumption of fixed capital can be measured directly or indirectly. The direct method is to conduct surveys of produced fixed assets at market at two consecutive periods and then calculate the decline in the market values of the stock of fixed assets. The indirect method recommended by SNA is the perpetual inventory method, which uses an approximation of market valuation and is less costly to implement. Depreciation in business accounting is not acceptable in national accounting since it is based on historical book values.

2.94.   Table T2.7 shows the difference between depreciation used in business accounting and consumption of fixed capital, which is the economic concept adopted by SNA. The very simple example given shows how depreciation in business accounts and consumption of fixed capital is calculated. It is assumed that the fixed asset was bought at time T-3 for 800 and entered in the business account at this price (e.g., book value or historical value), has a lifetime of four years and will be scrapped after that. The value of the fixed asset is assumed to decline proportionally over four years (straight line depreciation).

2.95.   Table T2.7, section 1, shows the calculation of depreciation in business or government accounting. Gross capital formation is recorded at book value. Since the asset survives four years, depreciation is simply calculated by dividing the book value by four.

2.96.   Table T2.7, section 2, shows the calculation of consumption of fixed capital by using the perpetual inventory method. The method requires first the calculation of gross capital stock and consumption of fixed capital at the base year price and then the inflating of these values into current prices by using price indexes. Thus, the following steps are required:

a)   The gross capital stock at book value is converted to the price of a base year. In this example, the base year is set at T-2;
b)   The consumption of fixed capital at the base year price is calculated by using the same straight -line depreciation assumption. Net capital stock at the base year price is the difference between gross capital stock and consumption of fixed capital;
c)   The next step is to derive consumption of fixed capital and net capital stock at current market values by using the price indexes.

TABLE T2.7. DEPRECIATION AND CONSUMPTION OF FIXED CAPITAL

1. Depreciation in business accounting at book value (straight line over 4 years)

		Calculating method	T_{-4}	T_{-3}	T_{-2}	T_{-1}	T	T_{+1}
1	Gross capital formation at book value (GCF)			800				
2	Depreciation at book value (D)	D= Line (1)/4		200	200	200	200	0
3	Net capital stock at book value, end of period[a]	NCS=NCS+GCF-D	0	600	400	200	0	0

2. Consumption of fixed capital in national accounting by the perpetual inventory method

		Calculating method	T_{-4}	T_{-3}	T_{-2}	T_{-1}	T	T_{+1}
4	Price index of fixed asset			100	105	106	115	
	At base year price of T_{-2}							
5	Gross capital formation (GCF)			840				
6	Consumption of fixed capital (CFC)	= Line (5)/4		210	210	210	210	0
7	Net capital stock, end of period	=NCS+ GCF-CFC	0	630	420	210	0	0
	At current market price							
8	Consumption of fixed capital at current market prices	=Line (6) price-adjusted by line (4)		200	210	212	230	0
9	Net capital stock at current market prices, end of period[a]	= Line (7) price-adjusted by line (4)		600	420	212	0	0

[a] By convention, depreciation and CFC start in the year in which GCF takes place.

2.97.   As can be seen in table T2.7, section 2, the calculation of the consumption of fixed capital of one fixed asset with a four-year lifetime at time T requires data on gross capital formation of that kind of asset from year T-3 on. The consumption of fixed capital of buildings with 30-year lifetime at the present time will require data on annual gross capital formation of buildings of the same kind for 30 years before that. Thus, the calculation of consumption of fixed capital requires long time-series of data on gross capital formation, their average service life and their probability of retirement. In practice, the compilation of net capital stock and the calculation of consumption of fixed capital require a combination of obtaining an initial benchmark estimate of capital stock (by survey) and a series of gross capital formation statistics.

2.98.   The simple method given in table T2.7 omits the effects of asset mortality, i.e., how assets are retired around the average service life, especially when there is more than one fixed asset of the same kind. The assumption of a straight-line depreciation may need to be replaced by a more realistic assumption that is appropriate for each kind of asset since some depreciate quickly at the beginning and slowly at the end of their service life, while the opposite is true for others.

2.99.   For more detailed information on the perpetual inventory method, readers are advised to consult the handbook *Links Between National Accounting and Business Accounting* (United Nations publishing, Sales No. or the OECD publication *Measuring Capital: A Manual on the OECD publication Measurement of Capital Stocks, Consumption of Fixed Capital and Capital Services* (Paris, 2001).

9. RELATIONSHIP BETWEEN CONSUMPTION OF FIXED CAPITAL, NET CAPITAL FORMATION, NET SAVING AND NET VALUE ADDED

2.100. Gross capital formation is the actual investment expense made to increase stocks of non-financial assets. However, part of it goes to replace the fixed assets that are used up in production. The using up of fixed assets is reflected in physical deterioration, normal obsolescence or normal accidental damages. Thus, the economic increase in fixed assets is net capital formation, which equals gross capital formation less consumption of fixed capital. Correspondingly, net value added and net saving are calculated by subtracting consumption of fixed capital from gross value added and gross saving.

EXERCISES ON GDP BY PRODUCTION AND FINAL EXPENDITURE

Given the attached information (which is highly simplified),

1. Estimate gross value added (VA) and VA/output ratio for each of the following industries by ISIC categories:

A+B	Agriculture, hunting, forestry and fishing
C	Mining and quarrying
D	Manufacturing
E	Electricity, gas and water supply
F	Construction
G+H	Wholesale, retail trade; repair of motor vehicles, motorcycles and personal and households goods; hotels and restaurants
I	Transport, storage and communications
J+K	Financial intermediation; real estate, renting and business services
L	Public administration and defense; compulsory social security
M+N+O	Education; health and social work; other community, social and personal services
P	Private households with employed persons

2. Estimate output, intermediate consumption (IC) and gross value added for non-market activities.
3. Estimate GDP by production approach.
4. Estimate final expenditure by type of expenditure:
   - Final consumption expenditure (C) for government, non-profit institutions serving households (NPISHs) and households
   - Gross capital formation (I)
   - Net exports (X-M)
5. Estimate GDP by expenditure and compare with GDP by production approach.

INFORMATION

A. Market output		
Industry	**Output** (Basic prices)	**Intermediate consumption** (Purchasers' prices)
Construction/repairs	300	250
Livestock	150	80
Forestry & fishing	280	96
Oil extraction	100	40
Garments	250	100
Other manufacturing	120	70
Electricity & water	40	15
Transport	145	86
Crops	450	140
Trade mark-up	230	90
Hotels & restaurants	120	55
Real estate	100	67
Business services	90	40
Private schools	40	23
Private hospitals	60	34
Recreation	50	30
Other personal services	100	60

B. Non-market economic activities	
Central and local government services	
Compensation of employees	200
Purchases of material and services (current expenditures only)	100
Consumption of fixed capital	60
Public schools and state colleges and universities (completely free)	
Compensation of employees	100
Purchases of materials and services (current expenditures only)	40
Consumption of fixed capital	10
Public hospitals (completely free)	
Compensation of employees	120
Purchases of material and services (current expenditures only)	70
Consumption of fixed capital	20
Non-government, churches and temples, others	
Compensation of employees	40
Purchases of materials and services (current expenditures only)	70
Consumption of fixed capital	5
C. Other estimated items	
Imputed value of owner-occupied dwelling units (based on equivalent market rent)	150
Purchases of materials and services for minor repairs	30
Residual	120
Consumption of own production of crops	70
D. Import taxes and other taxes on products less subsidies	250
E. Purchases of goods and services by households for consumption	950
F. Gross fixed capital formation	120
G. Change in inventory	20
H. Exports of goods and services f.o.b.	750
I. Imports of goods and services f.o.b.	600

Guides

- Non-profit institutions serving households (NPISHs) include non-market economic activities that are not mainly financed by government.
- Non-market activities that are mainly financed by the government should be classified into the general government sector.
- Output of general government and non-profit institutions serving households is calculated as the sum of compensation of employees, intermediate consumption and consumption of fixed capital.
- Final consumption expenditure of government includes output of government services less sales, plus output of other non-market activities financed by government (public schools and hospitals etc.) less sales, plus purchases of goods and services by government to be distributed free to households. Final consumption expenditure of NPISHs includes output of NPISHs less sales plus their purchases of goods and services to be distributed free to households. In the case that there is own-account gross capital formation, this own-account output has to be deducted from output to obtain final consumption expenditure.

SOLUTIONS

SOLUTIONS TO QUESTION 1

	Industry	Output	IC	VA	VA/O ratios
A+B	**Agriculture, hunting, forestry, fishing**	**880**	**316**	**564**	**.6409**
	Crops	450	140	310	.6889
	Livestock	150	80	70	.4667
	Forestry & fishing	280	96	184	.6571
C	**Mining and quarrying**	**100**	**40**	**60**	**.6000**
	Oil extraction	100	40	60	.6000
D	**Manufacturing**	**370**	**170**	**200**	**.5405**
	Garments	250	100	150	.6000
	Other manufacturing	120	70	50	.4167
E	**Electricity, gas and water supply**	**40**	**15**	**25**	**.6250**
F	**Construction, construction repairs**	**300**	**250**	**50**	**.1667**
G+H	**Wholesale, retail trade; repairs; hotels and restaurants**	**350**	**145**	**205**	**.5857**
	Trade mark-up	230	90	140	.6087
	Hotels & restaurants	120	55	65	.5417
I	**Transport, storage and communication**	**145**	**86**	**59**	**.4069**
J+K	**Financial intermediation; real estate, renting and business services**	**340**	**137**	**203**	**.5971**
	Imputed value of owner-occupied dwelling units (taken from part C)	150	30	120	.8000
	Real estate	100	67	33	.3300
	Business services	90	40	50	.5556
L	**Public administration and defense; compulsory social security**	**360**	**100**	**260**	**.7222**
	Central and local government non-market services (taken from part B)	360	100	260	.7222
M+N+O	**Education; health; other community, social and personal services**	**725**	**327**	**398**	**.5490**
	Public schools, state colleges and universities (taken from part B)	150	40	110	.7333
	Public hospitals (taken from part B)	210	70	140	.6667
	Private schools	40	23	17	.4250
	Private hospitals	60	34	26	.4333
	NGO, churches and temples, others (taken from part B)	115	70	45	.3913
	Recreation	50	30	20	.4000
	Other personal services	100	60	40	.4000
	TOTAL	**3610**	**1586**	**2024**	**.5607**

COMMENTS: Gross value added/output ratios are calculated for the base year when data on output, intermediate consumption and value added are all available through censuses or annual surveys; those ratios are then used to estimate gross value added thereafter when only data on output is available. (see part three for further discussion on the use of those ratios).

SOLUTION TO QUESTION 2

1. Output, intermediate consumption, gross value added of non-market activities			
	Output	**IC**	**VA**
Central and local government	**360**	**100**	**260**
Compensation of employees	200		200
Purchases of materials and services	100	100	
Consumption of fixed capital	60		60
Public schools and state colleges and universities	**150**	**40**	**110**
Compensation of employees	100		100
Purchases of materials and services	40	40	
Consumption of fixed capital	10		10
Public hospitals	**210**	**70**	**140**
Compensation of employees	120		120
Purchases of materials and services	70	70	
Consumption of fixed capital	20		20
Non-government, churches and temples	**115**	**70**	**45**
Compensation of employees	40		40
Purchases of materials and services	70	70	
Consumption of fixed capital	5		5

Comments:

1. The solution provides only "estimates", which are the best that one can obtain given the available information.

2. In computing output or intermediate consumption, one needs to have "use of materials and services", not "purchases of materials and services". On the one hand, part of the materials purchased may be put in inventory. On the other hand, materials may be withdrawn from the in inventory to be used in production. At any point in time, the following balance must be true:

> purchase of materials + beginning inventory of materials = use of materials + ending inventory of materials
> use of materials = purchase of materials - increase in inventory of materials

SOLUTION TO QUESTION 3

GDP by production approach:

GDP = total gross value added at basic prices + import taxes and other taxes on products less subsidies
= 2024 + 250 = 2274

SOLUTION TO QUESTION 4

Final consumption expenditure of the government (GFCE)

Final consumption expenditure of the government is equal to the sum of	**720**
Output of government services less sales	360
Less Own-account capital formation	0
Plus Other non-market services provided free by government (public schools & hospitals)	360
Plus Purchases of market goods and services to be distributed to households	0

Final consumption expenditure of non-profit institutions serving households (NPISHFCE)

Final consumption expenditure of NPISH is equal to the sum of	**115**
Output of NPISH services less sales	115
Less Own-account capital formation	0
Plus Purchases of market goods and services to be distributed free to households	0

Final consumption expenditure of households (HHFCE)

Final consumption expenditure of households is equal to the sum of	**1170**
Purchases of goods and services by households	950
Imputed value of owner-occupied housing	150
Consumption from own production of crops	70

Gross capital formation (GCF)

Gross capital formation	**140**
Gross fixed capital formation	120
Change in inventory	20
Acquisition less disposal of valuables	0

Net exports (X-M) = exports - imports

$$= \quad 750 - 600$$
$$= \quad 150$$

SOLUTION TO QUESTION 5

GDP by final expenditure approach

GDP   = final consumption expenditure + gross capital formation + net exports

GDP	=	GFCE + NPISHFCE + HHFCE + GCF + net exports
	=	720 + 115 +1170 +140 +150
	=	2295

Comparison of GDP by production and final expenditure approach

GDP by production approach:	2274
GDP by final expenditure approach:	2295
Difference:	21

If one assumes that GDP by production approach is more accurate, then the best GDP estimate is 2274 and 21 is considered statistical error. Thus:

GDP	=	2274
Final expenditure	=	2295
Statistical error	=	-21

The statistical error is 0.9 per cent of GDP.

In many developing countries, gross value added/output ratios that are derived from production survey on establishments for the base year are used to estimate value added. Those data are supplemented by actual annual data on large corporations, especially state-owned corporations and by data on government expenditures. Very few countries are financially capable of carrying out surveys on retail sale or even gross capital formation. Therefore, GDP based on the final expenditure approach is less reliable. In such situations, the production approach is more reliable than the final expenditure approach. In some countries, such as the United States, which can afford extensive surveys on final expenditure, the final expenditure approach is considered more reliable than those based on value added/output ratios. In other countries which can afford surveys on both production and final expenditure, it is not possible to know which is more reliable, as is the case in Canada. The statistical discrepancy is halved: one half is subtracted from the higher estimate of GDP and the other added to the lower estimate.

Chapter 3

Income account of the nation

A. OBJECTIVES

3.1.   The income account of the nation attempts to measure various forms of incomes of the nation. GDP is not an income concept but an aggregate measure of output of goods and services resulting from the production activity of all resident units within the borders of a country that are available for final uses.

3.2.   One important gross income concept of the nation is the net income (receipts less payments) received by resident units of the economy as a result of its ownership of factors of production (i.e., labour and capital, including financial and non-financial produced and non-produced capital). This is called **gross national income**.

3.3.   Another important gross income concept is **gross national disposable income,** which is the income that is available for final uses for the nation after redistribution of income between the economy and the rest of the world.

3.4.   The distribution and redistribution of income between domestic sectors of the economy (i.e., households, corporations, government) and between the economy and the rest of the world would have significant effects on the economic behaviour of those institutional sectors (that problem is discussed at the end of the present chapter; but for a thorough presentation on definitions of institutional sectors, see chap. 9). It is important to point out that for the total economy, the distribution and redistribution between domestic sectors will cancel each other out since a payment by one sector is a receipt by another. Only transactions with the rest of the world will have an effect on aggregate national income concepts.

B. IMPORTANT INCOME CONCEPTS

3.5.   The following are important income concepts in national accounts:

        a)   Primary income;
        b)   Gross national income;
        c)   Current transfers;
        d)   Gross national disposable income;
        e)   Gross saving.

C. PRIMARY INCOME

3.6.   Primary income is the kind of income derived from factors of production (i.e., labour and capital, including financial and non-financial produced and non-produced capital) and government power to tax.

3.7.   Primary income is generated in the production activity of resident producers and distributed mostly to other residents but also partly to non-residents. At the same time, residents receive primary income from the rest of the world.

3.8.   Primary income includes:

  a) Compensation of employees (labour cost);
  b) Taxes on production and imports;
  c) Mixed income: mixed income is the mixture of compensation of employees and operating surplus applied to the households that carry out economic activities but do not keep business accounts and therefore mix the payment to themselves and the operating surplus;
  d) Property income:
      i) Interest (excluding financial intermediation service charges indirectly measured – (FISIM);
      ii) Distributed income from corporations:
  e) Dividends;
  f) Withdrawals from income of quasi-corporations;[5]
      i) Reinvested earnings on direct foreign investments;[6]
      ii) Rent on land and sub-soil assets;
  g) Property income attributed to insurance policy holders.

D. GROSS NATIONAL INCOME

3.9.   Gross national income is the aggregate income of the nation generated by its production and its ownership of factors of production less the incomes paid out for the use of factors of production owned by the rest of the world.

3.10.   Gross national income is operationally defined in relation with GDP as follows (see also figure F3.1):

GNI = GDP + primary income receivable from the rest of the world (row) – primary income payable to the rest of the world

In more specific form:

GNI = GDP + compensation of employees and property income receivable from the rest of the world – compensation of employees and property income payable to the rest of world[7]

---

[5] This applies to sole proprietorships and partnerships, which are not independent legal entities, whose owners do not pay to themselves salaries but withdraw income from operating surplus and net property income for their own use.

[6] Undistributed to the rest of the world. The imputed distributed earnings are then imputed as additional financial investment. Shares of foreign investors as a consequence increase. That treatment affects the rest of the world account (or the balance of payment).

[7] The distribution of GDP in terms of compensation of employees, taxes on production and imports and property income among the domestic sectors will cancel each other out. Only transactions with the rest of the world remain. With respect to the rest of the world, the labour factor (in terms of compensation of employees) captures the production income that is generated by residents working temporarily outside of the country, such as seasonal workers, and the reduction in production income due to payment to temporary workers inside the country.

3.11. GNI was previously called **gross national product** (GNP). The reason for the change is that GNP is an income concept and not an output concept like GDP.

Figure T3.1. Relationship between GDP and gross national income

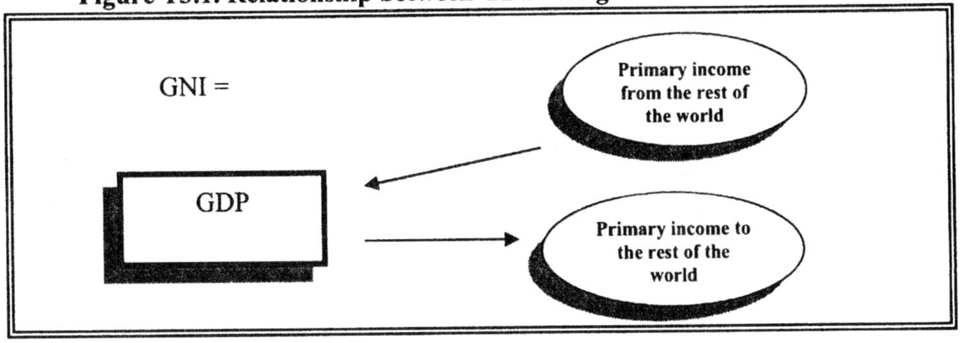

E. CURRENT TRANSFERS: TRANSACTIONS WITHOUT RECEIVING GOODS AND SERVICES IN RETURN

3.12. Current transfers are current transactions without receiving goods and services or capital in return as a counterpart in the same accounting period and not involving capital transfers.

3.13. Current transfers include:

    a) Social contributions to and benefits from social insurance schemes (see table T3.1),[8]
    b) Taxes on income;
    c) Net non-life insurance premiums (i.e., excluding insurance service charges, which are the output of non-life insurance services) and claims other than social insurance;
    d) International assistance for current uses;
    e) Immigrants' remittances;
    f) Other miscellaneous transfers.

F. GROSS NATIONAL DISPOSABLE INCOME

3.14. Gross national disposable income is the income available for final consumption of goods and services.

---

[8] Premiums paid to and benefits received from life insurance policies do not appear in the system. If they are part of group life insurance, premiums are included in social contributions and claims are included in social benefits from social insurance schemes. Individual life insurances (i.e., non-group) are considered part of the saving of households that is used to acquire financial assets; benefits are considered as a reduction in the financial assets of households. Thus, SNA does not show payment of premiums and receipts of claims of individual life insurance. The net transaction (premiums – claims – service charges) is treated as an increase in assets of households and an increase in liabilities of insurance companies. Property income generated from premiums by the insurance companies (insurance supplement) is treated as property attributable to insurance policy holders (i.e., households) from insurance companies. For a detailed discussion of treatment of insurance, social insurance and pension funds, see SNA, annex IV.

3.15. The difference between gross national disposable income and final consumption is gross saving (negative if final consumption is greater than disposable income).

FIGURE F3.2. RELATIONSHIP BETWEEN GROSS NATIONAL INCOME AND GROSS NATIONAL DISPOSABLE INCOME

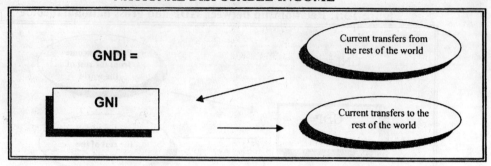

TABLE T3.1. CLASSIFICATION AND EXPLANATION OF SOCIAL CONTRIBUTIONS AND SOCIAL BENEFITS

Social insurance scheme must satisfy one of the following requirements: (a) participation is compulsory either by law or conditions of employment; (b) the scheme is operated on behalf of a group and restricted to group members; (c) an employer makes a contribution on behalf of an employee (for a detailed description of how social insurance schemes may include group pension, life and non-life insurances as well as how individual (i.e. non-group) life and non-life insurances are recorded in various accounts of SNA).

Social contributions by households		Social benefits to households	
1.1 Employers' actual social contribution:	This item is paid directly to organized social funds, such as social security funds, pension funds and insurance companies, for the benefit of employees. It is treated as part of compensation to employees and as an imputed item contributed by employees to social funds.	**2.1 Social benefits other than social transfers in kind**	Benefits received by households from the social schemes on the right side (1.1 to 1.4).
1.2 Employees' social contribution	Paid from employees' wages and salaries.	**2.12 Social security benefits in cash**	From social security funds
1.3 Social contribution by self-employed and non-employed persons	Contributions by households to organized social funds, such as social security funds.	**2.13 Private funded social benefits**	In cash or in kind paid by insurance companies or other institutional units administrating private funded social insurance schemes.
1.4 Imputed social contributions	This is an imputed item to account for the benefits employers are expected to pay directly to employees without going through organized social funds. It may be difficult to estimate those benefits and therefore it may be assumed to be the same as unfunded benefits (such as education grants, retirement benefits, medical payment not related to work etc.) paid to employees shown on the right side (2.14).	**2.14 Unfunded employees social benefits**	In cash or in kind. (see explanation under 1.4 on the right side).
		2.15 Social assistance benefits in cash	Payments by government or non-profit institutions which are not received from social insurance schemes.

FIGURE F3.3 DERIVATION OF GROSS SAVING

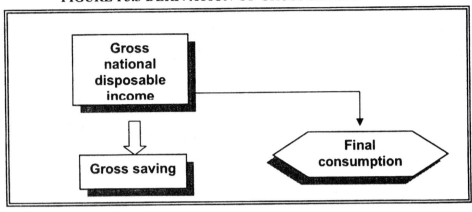

G. RELATION BETWEEN INCOME OF INSTITUTIONAL SECTORS AND THE TOTAL ECONOMY

3.16.   The distribution and redistribution of incomes between sectors (i.e., the government sector, the household sector, the non-financial corporations, the financial corporations and the rest of the world) have significance for the formation of gross disposable income that can be used for either final consumption, saving or capital formation of each sector. Table T3.2, which is extracted from table T3.3, shows that households obtain income from their own production activities (gross value added) and from being employed in the labour market (compensation of employees) and property income by investing in the financial market, and must also pay out taxes and property income. The balance of primary income, which makes up the gross national income, is 170. Also, owing to the receipt of social benefits and current transfers net of the payments of income taxes, social contributions and other current transfers, the gross disposable income of households is 182. Gross disposable income may be significantly higher than the balance of primary income.

TABLE T3.2 HOUSEHOLD INCOME

	Uses	Resources
Gross value added at basic prices		32
Compensation of employees	0	131
Other taxes less subsidies on production	1	
Property income	2	10
Balance of primary income	**170**	
Balance of primary income		**170**
Current taxes on income	50	
Social contributions	40	
Social benefits other than in kind		101
Other current transfers	20	21
Gross disposable income	**182**	

3.17.   The distribution and redistribution of income between domestic sectors do not affect gross national income (GNI) and gross national disposable income (GNDI) since a receipt by one sector cancels out a payment by the other. That is why GNI can be calculated by a simple formula: GNI= GDP+ compensation of employees and property income receivable from the rest of the world - compensation of employees and property income payable to the rest of the world. (GNI = 216+3+3-

5=217). Gross national disposable income is similarly calculated by adding to GNI net current transfers from the rest of the world. (GNDI (226) = GNI (217) + (10-1)).

3.18.   In table T3.3, the integrated accounts show the sequence of accounts of each institutional sector separately in two columns: uses (U) and resources (R). The balancing item at the end of each account on the left side is derived as a difference between the sum of sources and the sum of uses. The balancing item then becomes resources on the right side of each account. For example, for the household sector, the balance of primary income is equal to (32+131+10)-(1+2)=170. The accounts of the total economy are the sum of the accounts of the sectors, line by line. The table is a condensed version of SNA for illustration purposes: it combines the generation of income account and the allocation of primary income in one account (for example of the full integrated account, see annex). The following should be noted:

a) In line 1, under "Total economy", the figure 216 is GDP, which is the sum of gross value added at basic prices of all institutional sectors (196=146+12+6+32) and taxes less subsidies on products (20) (the latter is not shown in the table);

b) In line 3, in all institutional sectors, the values paid out (i.e., on the use side) are "other taxes on production" only. For the total economy on the use side, taxes less subsidies (20) are added to "other taxes on production" (3) to obtain "taxes less subsidies on production and imports" (23). The whole value of "taxes less subsidies on production and imports" (23) is received by the government on the resource side;

c) In line 14, net equity of households in pension funds contributed as social contributions is kept in the accounts of financial institutions. In order to show the actual gross saving of the households, the adjustment imputes a payment from the financial sector to the household sector. It is assumed here that pension funds are managed by the financial sector. In reality, pension funds may be managed by the government.

TABLE T3.3. NATIONAL AND SECTORAL INCOMES IN THE INTEGRATED ACCOUNTS

	Non-financial corporations		Financial corporations		Government		Household		Total economy		Rest of the world sector		Totals checking	
	U	R	U	R	U	R	U	R	U	R	U	R	U	R
ALLOCATION OF PRIMARY INCOME														
1 Gross value added/GDP		146		12		6		32		216			196	216
2 Compensation of employees	120		7		6			131	133	131	3	5	136	136
3 Taxes less subsidies on production and imports	2		0		0	23		1	23	23				
4 Property income	14	11	10	8	4	4	2	10	30	33	3	0	33	33
5 Balance of primary income/gross national income	21		3		23		170		217					
SECONDARY DISTRIBUTION OF INCOME														
6 Balance of primary income/National income		21		3		23		170		217				
7 Current taxes on income	8		1			59	50		59	59			59	59
8 Social contributions				30		10	40		40	40			40	40
9 Social benefits other than in kind	1		40		60			101	101	101			101	101
10 Other current transfers			9	20	3		20	21	32	41	10	1	42	42
11 Gross disposable income/GNDI	12		3		29		182		226					
USES OF DISPOSABLE INCOME														
12 Gross disposable income/GNDI		12		3		29		182		226				
13 Final consumption expenditures	0		0		11		152		163					
14 Adjustment for change in net equity of households in pension funds			10					10	10	10				
15 Gross saving	12		-7		18		40		63					

49

EXERCISE ON GROSS NATIONAL INCOME, GROSS NATIONAL DISPOSABLE INCOME AND GROSS SAVING

Given GDP, final consumption and the information on the current account of the balance of payments provided below, identify primary income, current transfers and estimate gross national income, disposable income and saving.

Information

GDP = 2224

Final consumption = Final consumption expenditure of the government

+ Final consumption expenditure of non-profit institutions serving households

+ Final consumption expenditure of households

= 2145

Current account	Credit (receivable)	Debit (payable)
A. Goods and services		
Exports	550	
Imports		600
B. Income		
Compensation of employees		10
Direct investment income		
Income on equity (dividends)		30
Income on debt (interest)	5	40
Porfolio investment		
Investment on equity (dividends)		15
Investment on debt (interest)		20
Other investment		
Interest		
Imputed income to households from net equity in life insurance and pension funds	1	3
C. Current transfers		
General government (grants current expenditure)	100	
Other sectors		
Workers' remittances	200	
Other transfers	20	5

SOLUTION

Primary income

	Receivable	Payable
Primary income	6	118
Compensation of employees		10
Other taxes less subsidies on production		
Property income	6	108
Dividends		45
Interest	5	60
Net equity in insurance & pension	1	3

Gross national income

Gross national income = GDP
+ Primary income receivable
- Primary income payable
-
= 2224 + 6 - 118
= 2112

Current transfers

	Receivable	Payable
Current transfers	320	5

Gross national disposable income (GNDI)

GNDI = Gross national income
+ Current transfers receivable
- Current transfers payable

= 2112 + 320 - 5
= 2427

Gross saving

Gross saving = Gross national disposable income - Final consumption
= 2427 - 2145
= 282

- **Comments:** Given the information in the balance of payments (BOP) without details, estimates of primary income and therefore gross national income are inexact. The reasons are: (1) other taxes less subsidies on production are classified as part of current transfers in BOP; (2) implicit financial service charges were either included in or deducted from interest, so they must be adjusted to get the true income flows. See *Links between Business Accounting and National Accounting* (United Nations publication, Sales No.E.00.XVII.13), chap. I.

Chapter 4

Capital account of the nation

A. OBJECTIVES

4.1.   The capital account attempts to identify investment in non-financial assets and the funds that can be used to finance them.

4.2.   Funds come from:

a) Gross saving (internal source);
b) Net capital transfers (received less paid), which are the external source of funds without a return of goods and service to the counterpart, such as grants from the rest of the world for the purpose of gross capital formation;
c) Net borrowing or net lending from the rest of the world.

4.3.   Investment in non-financial assets includes:

a) Gross capital formation;
b) Net acquisition of non-produced non-financial assets from the rest of the world.[9]

4.4.   The capital account also attempts to identify new or additions to capital assets by the following types (for a more complete classification of assets, see table T2.3):

a) Dwellings;
b) Other buildings and structures;
  i)   Non-residential buildings;
  ii) Other structures;
c) Machinery and equipment:
  i)   Transport equipment;
  ii) Other machinery and equipment;
d) Cultivated assets:
  i)   Livestock for breeding, dairy, draught etc.;
  ii) Vineyards, orchards and other plantations of trees yielding repeat products;
e) Mineral exploration;
f) Computer software;
g) Entertainment, literary or artistic originals;
h) Other intangible fixed assets.

4.5.   Net lending / net borrowing from the rest of the world can be derived by the following formula (see table T4.1 for the relationships):

---

[9] See the exception rule given below figure F4.1.

net lending (+) or net borrowing (-) = gross capital formation + net acquisition of non-produced assets - (gross saving + net capital transfers)

FIGURE F4.1. GROSS CAPITAL FORMATION

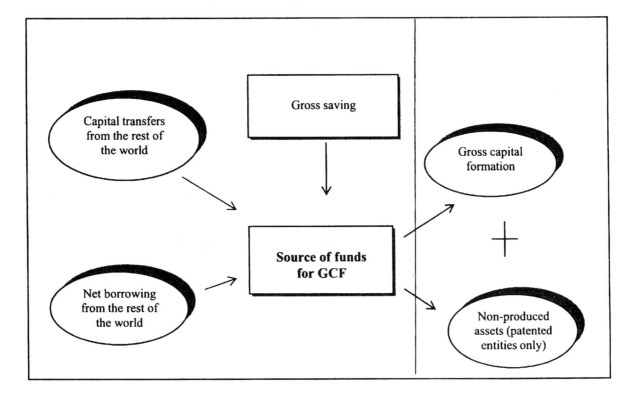

Exception rule: SNA assures that transactions of produced fixed assets, such as buildings, and other non-produced assets, such as land, sub-soil assets and legal constructs (leases etc.) between residents of a national economy and the rest of the world are effected between residents since those assets remain in the economy and serve the production activities in the economy. As a result, SNA creates a notional resident unit, representing non-residents, that owns them. Since transactions among residents cancel each other out (a purchase cancels out a sale), changes in non-produced assets above include only intangible non-produced assets, such as patented entities. Purchases of those assets by non-residents are treated as purchases of financial assets.

B. INVESTMENT IN NON-FINANCIAL ASSETS AND SOURCES OF FUNDS

4.6.   The relationship between resources and uses in the capital account is described in table T4.1.

TABLE T4.1 RELATIONSHIP BETWEEN RESOURCES AND USES IN THE CAPITAL ACCOUNT

Uses	Resources
• Gross capital formation	• Gross saving
• Acquisition less disposal of non-financial, non-produced assets from rest of the world	• Net capital transfers are without-a- counterpart transfers from the rest of the world, such as investment grants (see box below)
Net lending (+) or Net borrowing (-) from rest of the world	

C. GROSS SAVING

4.7.   From the SNA point of view, gross saving includes consumption of fixed capital (similar to depreciation but revalued at market prices).

4.8.   From the business point of view, gross saving includes depreciation (funds treated by business as cost of production but in fact set aside as a source of funds for investment).

4.9.   Gross saving in SNA is not the same as gross saving from the business point of view since consumption of fixed capital is not the same as depreciation.

Capital transfers: Capital transfers differ from current transfers in that they involve the acquisition or disposal of assets by at least one party of the transaction. Capital transfers can be in cash or in kind. They include:

- **Capital taxes** levied at irregular intervals on the value of assets or net worth owned by institutional sectors or transferred as gifts, legacies or inheritance.
- **Investment grants** in cash or in kind (grants by government for interest relief, even for encouraging GCF, are excluded; they include, however, the financing of GCF and also the payment of interest).
- **Other capital transfers,** such as payment to owners of capital destroyed by political events or natural calamities, payment to cover losses accumulated over several years, transfers between government units to cover unexpected expenditure or accumulated deficits, non-recurrent bonus payment to households to reward savings carried out over a number of years, cancellation of debts by agreement, payment in compensation of extensive damages not covered by insurance policies, extraordinary payment by government or employers to increase the actuarial reserve of social insurance funds and redistribution of realized capital gains from insurance companies to households.

Chapter 5

Financial account of the nation

A. OBJECTIVES

5.1.   The financial account of the nation, also known as the flow of funds when extended to cover flows between various sectors, attempts to identify "investment" in financial instruments, debts and forms of debts, as well as to derive net lending or net borrowing.

5.2.   The difference between the total change in financial assets and the total change in liabilities is net lending if the difference is positive and net borrowing if it is negative (see table T5.1).

5.3.   The account shows (a) how net borrowing of the nation was carried out, either by incurring liabilities or reducing financial assets, and in what type of financial instrument, or (b) how net lending operated, either by acquiring financial assets or reducing liabilities, and in what type of financial instrument.

TABLE T5.1. RELATIONSHIP BETWEEN CHANGES IN FINANCIAL ASSETS AND LIABILITIES

Assets	Liabilities
Net lending (+) / Net borrowing (-)	
• Change in financial assets:	• Change in financial liabilities:
Monetary gold and SDRs	
Currency and deposits Currency Transferable deposits Other deposits	Currency and deposits Currency Transferable deposits Other deposits
Securities other than shares (like bonds, bills, certificates of deposits, commercial papers, debentures, etc.) Short-term Long-term	Securities other than shares (like bonds, bills, certificates of deposits, commercial papers, debentures, etc.) Short-term Long-term
Loans Short-term Long-term	Loans Short-term Long-term
Shares and other equity (like stocks, foreign direct investment, etc.)	Shares and other equity (like stocks, foreign direct investment, etc.)
Insurance technical reserves (net equity in pension and life insurance funds)	Insurance technical reserves (net equity in pension and life insurance funds)
Financial derivatives	Financial derivatives
Other accounts receivable Trade credits and advances Others	Other accounts payable Trade credits and advances Others

B. DEFINITION OF ASSETS AND LIABILITIES

5.4.   An economic asset is a store of value over which ownership rights are enforced, individually or collectively, and from which the owner may derive economic benefits by holding it or using it over a period of time. Economic benefits include primary income and possible holding gains or loss due to change in the prices of assets. An economic asset may be in the form of buildings, currency, securities, shares and other equity, loans and accounts receivable.

5.5.   Liability is a debt, an amount owed to creditors, a financial obligation or a claim against assets. Domestic currency, for example, is a financial liability or obligation of the central bank that issues it, and an asset of those who hold it. A provider of loan holds an asset of loan against those who borrow and who thus have a liability to the provider of the loan.

5.6.   Transactions in financial assets are recorded at the prices at which the assets are acquired or disposed of, excluding service charges, fees or commissions provided in carrying out the transactions. Those costs of changes in ownership are recorded as purchases of financial services, a part of intermediate consumption, in the production accounts of the transactors who pay. That treatment is different from that of costs of changes in ownership of non-financial assets.

5.7.   A financial asset always has a financial liability as a counterpart except for gold that is used as money or for special drawing rights (SDRs) issued by the International Monetary Fund.

5.8.   In the account, an increase in a liability or an asset is recorded as a positive value, while a reduction in a liability (for example, payment or repurchase) or an asset is recorded as a negative value.

5.9.   The financial account records only changes in financial assets and liabilities. Stocks of liabilities and financial assets are recorded in the balance sheets.

5.10.   Since the financial account of the nation records only changes in liabilities and financial assets by types, it does not reveal the flow of funds from one institutional sector to another, as is the case in the integrated financial accounts of the institutional sectors.

C. RELATION WITH THE CAPITAL ACCOUNT

5.11.   The financial account records changes in financial assets on the left and in financial liabilities on the right. The difference between the totals is either net lending (+) or net borrowing (-) from the rest of the world.

5.12.   Net lending / net borrowing of the financial account and the capital account are independently calculated, but in principle they must be the same.

5.13.   Net lending / net borrowing calculated from the total economy must be equal to net lending / net borrowing calculated from the rest of the world in absolute value but opposite sign.

TABLE T5.2. FINANCIAL ACCOUNT OF THE NATION: AN EXAMPLE

Assets		Liabilities	
Net lending (+)/borrowing (-)	-100		
• Change in financial assets:	-50	• Change in financial liabilities:	50
○ Foreign currencies	-30	○ Loans	50
○ Foreign share	-20		

Note: Net borrowing of a country (100 in this instance) can take many forms: an increase in liabilities (for example, loans) to foreign countries, a reduction in the holding of foreign assets (for example, foreign currencies, stocks) or a combination of the two.

EXERCISE ON CLASSIFICATION OF TRANSACTIONS

- Economic flows reflect the creation, transformation, exchange, transfer or extinction of economic value. Economic flows are of two kinds: transactions and other flows.

- **A transaction** is an economic flow that is an interaction between institutional units by mutual agreement or an action within an institutional unit that it is analytically useful to treat like a transaction.

- Transactions may be in the form of:
    - Goods and services.
    - Income (distributive).
    - Financial instruments.

- **Other flows** are changes in the value of assets and liabilities that do not take place in transactions.

- The compilation of different accounts requires an appropriate classification of transactions and other flows. The following exercise requires the classification of the information given below in the following categories: output, intermediate consumption, primary income (compensation of employees, other taxes on production, property income), current transfers, gross capital formation, acquisition less disposal of non-produced assets, change in financial asset, change in financial liability (by detailed items).

Information

	Principal party	Counterpart party
A household pays $500 for the electric bill to the electric company	Final consumption expenditure	Output
A household produces 2 tons of rice for own consumption		
$2 million grant is received from Japan for the construction of a bridge		
Households buy thread worth $10 from a corporation to be used for weaving of cloth		
A corporation pays corporate income taxes		
A joint venture reinvests its earnings in the country		
A corporation purchases materials for production, with a promise to pay the following year		
Households receive money gift from relatives abroad		
Households receive consumer goods as gift from relatives abroad		
A corporation is supposed to pay interest to a bank but is unable to pay and the interest is not written off		
Loss realized due to a decline in the stock market		
Gain realized in selling a house		
A corporation pays rent on a building it rents		
A corporation pays rent on a piece of land it rents		
A corporation issues bonds		

NOTE: It is important to recognize that the correct classification of transactions is crucial in national accounting. A transaction which is intermediate consumption, if incorrectly classified as property income, will increase GDP, and vice versa.

SOLUTION

	Principal party	Counterpart party
A household pays $500 for the electric bill to the electric company	Final consumption expenditure	Output
A household produces 2 tons of rice for own consumption	Final consumption expenditure	Output
$2 million grant is received from Japan for the construction of a bridge	Capital transfer receivable, output	Capital transfer payable, Output, gross capital formation
Households buy thread worth $10 from a corporation to be used for weaving of cloth	Intermediate consumption	Output
A corporation pays corporate income taxes	Current transfer	Current transfer
Joint venture reinvests its earnings in the country	Dividend receivable and increase in share (asset)	Dividend payable and increase in share (liability)
A corporation purchases materials for production, with a promise to pay the following year	Intermediate consumption, increase in account payable (liability)	Output, increase in account receivable (asset)
Households receive money gift from relatives abroad	Current transfer	Current transfer
Households receive consumer goods as gift from relatives abroad	Current transfer, imports of goods, final consumption expenditure	Current transfer, exports of goods
A corporation is supposed to pay interest to a bank but is unable to pay and the interest is not written off	Property income payable, accounts payable (liability)	Property income receivable, accounts receivable (asset)
Loss realized due to a decline in the stock market	Other flow (revaluation of financial assets)	
Gain realized in selling a house	Other flow (revaluation of non-financial assets)	
A corporation pays rent on a building it rents	Intermediate consumption (rental in the SNA)	Output
A corporation pays rent on a piece of land it rents	Property income (rent in the SNA)	Property income
A corporation issues bonds	Increase in securities other than shares (liability)	Increase in securities other than shares (asset)

Chapter 6

Rest of the world account

A. OBJECTIVES

6.1.   The rest of the world account identifies:

   a) Deficit or surplus with the rest of the world in trade in goods and services, current transactions and net lending (+) or net borrowing (-);
   b) Capital and financial transactions with the rest of the world;
   c) The international investment position, i.e., the holding of financial assets and liabilities vis-à-vis the rest of the world, essentially debt;
   d) Conceptually, the rest of the world account is the same as the balance of payments and has the same sub-accounts, but its sub-accounts are aggregated differently for different purposes;
   e) The present chapter explains the transactions with the rest of the world, the major balances in the account, and the relation between the rest of the world account and trade statistics.

B. TRANSACTIONS WITH THE REST OF THE WORLD

6.2   A transaction between the domestic institutional sectors and the rest of the world is a transaction between residents of an economic territory and non-residents.

6.3   A transaction of goods and services from residents to non-residents is an export and from non-residents to residents is an import (see also definition of residents and non-residents and exports and imports of goods and services provided in paras. 2.48-2.59 above.

6.4   Other current transactions include property incomes and other current transfers.

6.5   Capital transfers are transactions in which the provider provides a good, a service or asset to another unit without receiving in return from the latter any counterpart in the form of a good, service or asset.

6.6   Financial transactions include all transactions between domestic sectors and the rest of the world that increase or reduce their financial assets and liabilities. A deposit in a bank in the rest of the world increases the financial asset of the economy and the financial liability of the rest of the world. A payment to reduce the principal of a loan from the rest of the world reduces the financial liability of the economy and the financial asset of the rest of the world.

C. BALANCES IN THE REST OF THE WORLD ACCOUNT

6.7   The balances in the rest of the world account may be illustrated as follows:

• Exports less imports	⟹	• Trade balance of goods and services
• Trade balance + net primary income from the rest of the world + net current transfers from the rest of the world	⟹	• Current external balance
• Current external balance + net capital transfers from the rest of the world	⟹	• Net borrowing (-) or net lending (+) from/to the rest of the world
• Financial transactions (changes in assets and liabilities) with the rest of the world	⟹	• Net borrowing (-) or net lending (+) from/to the rest of the world
• Assets and liabilities with the rest of the world	⟹	• Change in net worth vis-à-vis the rest of the world or change in international financial position

D. RELATION BETWEEN TRADE STATISTICS AND TRADE BALANCE OF GOODS AND SERVICES

6.8.   Trade statistics cover only imports and exports of goods crossing borders.

6.9.   SNA and the balance of payments record change of ownership and therefore also include goods and services that do not cross borders as long as they are transactions between residents and non-residents (except for non-produced assets and buildings located in the country).

6.10.   SNA values exports and imports of goods f.o.b.

6.11.   Imported goods are normally valued c.i.f., that is, including freight and insurance (F&I) to bring goods to destination.

6.12.   A part of freight and insurance services may be provided by residents (domestic output of services) and another by non-residents (imported services). Therefore, when imports of goods are valued c.i.f., they also include some domestic services of freight and insurance.

6.13.   When imports are valued f.o.b., that is, when freight and insurance services on imported goods are excluded, imports contain only values of goods.

6.14.   Exports are always valued f.o.b. in trade statistics and national accounts.

6.15.   Exports and imports of services must be separately collected and then added to exports and imports of goods in order to arrive at total exports and imports of goods and services. In addition, illegal exports and imports and exports of goods and services not crossing borders between residents and non-residents must also be estimated to add in the totals.

TABLE T6.1. REARRANGEMENT OF TRADE STATISTICS INTO THE REST OF THE WORLD ACCOUNT: AN EXAMPLE

Trade statistics			Rest of the world account		
Imported goods c.i.f.		26	Imports of goods f.o.b.		23
Goods f.o.b.	23		Equal Imports of goods c.i.f.	26	
F&I provided by residents	1		Less F&I on imported goods	-3	
F&I provided by non-residents	2				
Imports of other services			Imports of other services		10
Exports of goods		30	Exports of goods and services		38
			Balance of trade		5

Chapter 7

Balance sheet of the nation

A. OBJECTIVES

7.1.   The balance sheet:

    a) Takes stock of the type and value of all financial and non-financial assets and liabilities (debts) of the economy at the beginning and end of the year;

    b) Identifies the changes in net worth and their sources leading to the "net wealth" of the nation.

7.2.   The stock of fixed assets, as part of the balance sheet, is an important statistic for studying and planning economic growth.

B. COMPONENTS OF BALANCE SHEET

7.3.   The difference between the closing balance sheet and the opening balance sheet is the changes in the balance sheet. Changes are the results of four factors that occur during the accounting period:

    a) **Gross capital formation and change in non-produced assets:** changes that are the direct result of production activities of the nation and transactions in capital goods and services;

    b) **Net acquisition of financial assets:** changes that are the result of financial transactions in the economy and with the rest of the world;

    c) **Other changes in volume:** changes that are due to such factors as discoveries or the depletion of natural, unproduced resources, such as minerals, or destruction by war and natural catastrophes;

    d) **Other changes due to revaluation:** changes that are due to changes in the prices of assets, which are reflected in holding gains and losses.

FIGURE F7.1. BALANCE SHEET OF THE NATION

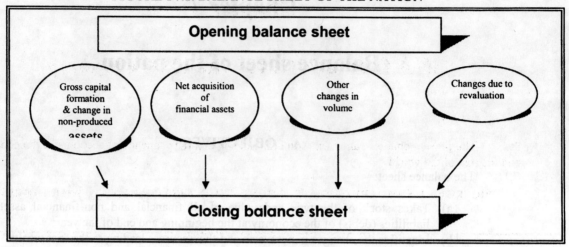

C. NET WORTH

7.4.   Net worth of the nation is equal to the total value of assets less the total value of liabilities.

7.5.   Change in the net worth can be broken down into three components:

   a) Change due to transactions (gross capital formation and net acquisition of non-produced and financial assets);
   b) Change due to changes in volume (natural discovery, destruction, inventions);
   c) Change due to increase/decrease in prices (revaluation).

Chapter 8

SNA framework for the total economy

8.1   The present chapter summarizes the relationships in the sequence of accounts of the economy and the rest of the world.

FIGURE F8.1. SUMMARY OF TRANSACTIONS WITHIN THE ECONOMY AND WITH THE REST OF THE WORLD

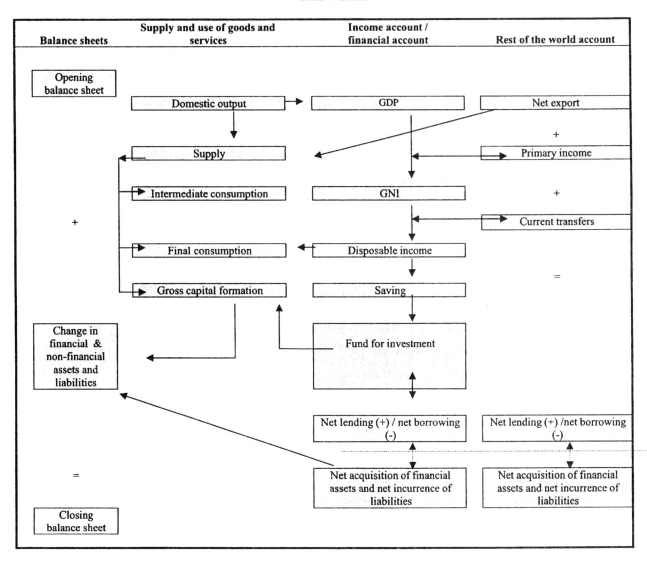

8.2.   Figure F8.1 summarizes the transactions within the economy and with the rest of the world. The four columns in the figure represent the different SNA accounts: the balance sheet; the supply and use of goods and services (which can be used to derive the production and capital accounts); generation, distribution and use of income accounts; and the rest of the world account. Flows and uses of incomes are shown to affect different accounts of the total economy. Below the broken line in the income and rest of the world accounts, net lending / net borrowing can be independently derived by taking the difference between net acquisition of financial assets and net incurrence of liabilities. See also figure F1.1.

8.3.   Table T8.1 gives an example of a condensed sequence of accounts of the total economy and the rest of the world. The full sequence of accounts, with all institutional sectors of the economy, is contained in the annex. Institutional sectors are explained in part two. For convenience of comparison, the numbering of the table in the annex is kept, except for lines 1-19, due to the fact that many intermediate accounts have been dropped from the abbreviated sequence of accounts. The column checking is designed to verify whether the total use is equal to the total resource for each appropriate line. The total is the sum of the rest of the world and the total economy.

TABLE T8.1. AN EXAMPLE OF THE FULL SEQUENCE OF ACCOUNTS OF THE TOTAL ECONOMY AND THE RELATION WITH THE REST OF THE WORLD

		Rest of the world sector		Total economy		Totals checking	
		(5)		(6)		(7)	
		U	R	U	R	U	R
	PRODUCTION ACCOUNTS						
1	Imports f.o.b.		28				
2	Exports f.o.b.	41					
3	External balance of goods & services	-13					
4	Output at basic prices				376		
5	Intermediate consumption			180			
6	Gross value added at basic prices			196			
7	Compensation of employees			133			
8	Wages and salaries			121			
9	Employers social contributions			12			
10	Other taxes on production			3			
11	Gross operating surplus			29			
12	Gross mixed income			31			
13	Taxes less subsidies on products			20			
14	GDP			216			
	ALLOCATION OF PRIMARY INCOME						
15	External balance of goods & services		-13				
16	GDP				216		
17	Compensation of employees	3	5	133	131	136	136
18	Property income	3	0	30	33	33	33
19	Gross national income			217			

		Rest of the world sector		Total economy		Totals checking	
		(5)		(6)		(7)	
		U	R	U	R	U	R
	SECONDARY DISTRIBUTION OF INCOME						
27	Balance of primary income/Gross national income				217		
28	Current taxes on income			59	59	59	59
29	Social contributions			40	40	40	40
30	Social benefits other than in kind			101	101	101	101
31	Other current transfers	10	1	32	41	42	42
32	**Gross national disposable income**			226			
	USES OF DISPOSABLE INCOME						
38	Gross disposable income				226		
39	Final consumption expenditures			163			
42	**Gross saving**			63			
43	**Current external balance**	-23					
	CAPITAL ACCOUNTS						
45	Gross saving				63		
46	Current external balance		-23				
47	Gross capital formation			40			
48	Consumption of fixed capital			12			
49	Net capital formation			28			
50	Acquisition less disposal of non-produced assets			0			
51	Capital transfers, receivable				2		2
52	Capital transfers, payable		-1		-1		-2
53	**Net lending (+) / Net borrowing (-)**	-24		24			
	FINANCIAL ACCOUNTS						
54	**Net lending (+) / Net borrowing (-)**		-24		24		0
55	Net acquisition of financial assets	-4		110		106	
56	Net incurrence of financial liabilities		20		86		106
57	Currency and deposits and the like	-1	2	14	11	13	13
58	Securities other shares	-2	7	32	23	30	30
59	Loans	0	8	31	23	31	31
60	Shares and other equity	-3	3	10	4	7	7
61	Insurance technical reserves, net equity	0	0	18	18	18	18
66	Other accounts receivable/payable	2	0	5	7	7	7

	Rest of the world sector (5)		Total economy (6)		Totals checking (7)	
	U	R	U	R	U	R
BALANCE SHEETS						
OPENING BALANCE SHEETS						
67 Non-financial assets	0		1131			
68 Produced assets			611			
69 Non-produced assets			520			
70 Financial assets/liabilities	54	25	624	600	678	625
71 **Opening net worth**		29		1155		1184
CHANGE IN THE BALANCE SHEETS from						
CAPITAL AND FINANCIAL ACCOUNTS						
72 Non-financial assets	0		28			
73 Produced assets	0		28			
74 Non-produced assets	0		0			
75 Financial assets/liabilities	-4	20	110	86	106	106
OTHER CHANGES IN VOLUME & REVALUATION						
76 Non-financial assets			100			
77 Produced assets			56			
78 Non-produced assets			44			
79 Financial assets/liabilities	4	0	27	18	31	18
Change in net worth		-20		161		141
80 Gross saving		-23		63		
81 Consumption of fixed capital		0		-12		
82 Capital transfers		-1		1		
83 Other changes in volume and revaluation		4		109		113
CLOSING BALANCE SHEETS						
84 Non-financial assets	0		1259			
85 Produced assets	0		695			
86 Non-produced assets	0		564			
87 Financial assets/liabilities	54	45	761	704	815	749
88 **Closing net worth**		9		1316		1325

68

EXERCISE ON SETTING UP A FULL SYSTEM OF ACCOUNTS OF THE NATION

Given the following information on an economy for the year 2000, set up the accounts according to the table provided on the following page.

Information

1. Items in the balance sheet at the end of the year 1999 are as follows:

   Value of all non-financial assets (buildings, roads, machinery etc.): 1000
   Loans provided by resident sectors (total asset): 100
       Of which loans provided to the rest of the world: 10
   Loans liable by resident sectors (total liabilities): 240
       Of which loans liable to the rest of the world: 150
   Domestic currency (stock): 200

2. Output (at basic prices) produced in the year 2000: 450
3. Taxes less subsidies on products: 20
4. Intermediate consumption used in production: 300
5. Final consumption: 190
6. Consumption of fixed capital: 5
7. Purchase of machinery: 50

8. Exports: 30
9. Imports: 100

10. Investment grant received from abroad: 2

11. Interest paid to abroad: 10
12. Interest received from the rest of the world: 2

13. New loans issued by resident sectors to other residents: 20
14. New loans owed to the rest of the world: 76

15. New issue of currency: 10
16. Increase in the value of non-financial assets due to inflation: 30

Notes:

- Not all information on the economy is given, for example, property income paid to residents.
- The rest of the world accounts must be set up from the point of view of the rest of the world.
- Make sure that net lending / net borrowing is the same for the capital account and the financial account.
- Make sure that net lending / net borrowing of the total economy and the rest of the world are the same in absolute value but opposite in sign.

Total economy account		Rest of the world	
Output at basic prices		Exports	
Intermediate consumption		Imports	
Gross value added at basic prices		**Balance of trade**	
Taxes less subsidies on products			
GDP			
Property income receivable		Property income receivable	
Property income payable		Property income payable	
Gross national income (GNI)			
Current transfer receivable			
Current transfer payable			
Gross national disposable income			
Final consumption			
Gross saving		**Balance of current account**	
Capital transfer receivable		Capital transfer receivable	
Capital transfer payable		Capital transfer payable	
Gross capital formation			
Net lending (+) / Net borrowing		**Net lending (+) / Net borrowing**	
Change in financial assets		Change in financial assets	
Currency		Currency	
Loans		Loans	
Change in financial liabilities		Change in financial liabilities	
Currency		Currency	
Loans		Loans	
Net lending (+) / Net borrowing		**Net lending (+) / Net borrowing**	
Opening balance sheet (end of 1999)		**Opening balance sheet (end of 1999)**	
Non-financial assets			
Financial assets		Financial assets	
Currency		Currency	
Loans		Loans	
Financial liabilities		Financial liabilities	
Currency		Currency	
Loans		Loans	
Net worth		Net worth	
Change in balance sheet		**Change in balance sheet**	
Non-financial assets			
Gross capital formation			
Consumption of fixed capital			
Holding gain			
Financial assets		Financial assets	
Financial liabilities		Financial liabilities	
Change in net worth		Change in net worth	
Ending balance sheet (end of 2000)		**Ending balance sheet (end of 2000)**	
Non-financial assets			
Financial assets		Financial assets	
Financial liabilities		Financial liabilities	
Net worth		Net worth	
Change in net worth		**Change in net worth**	

SOLUTION

Total economy account			Rest of the world	
Output at basic prices		450	Exports	-30
Intermediate consumption		-300	Imports	100
Gross value added at basic prices		150	**Balance of trade**	70
Taxes less subsidies on products		20		
GDP		170		
Property income receivable		2	Property income receivable	-2
Property income payable		-10	Property income payable	10
Gross national income (GNI)		162		
Current transfer receivable		0		
Current transfer payable		0		
Gross national disposable income		162		
Final consumption		-190		
Gross saving		-28	**Balance of current account**	78
Capital transfer receivable		2	Capital transfer receivable	-2
Capital transfer payable		0	Capital transfer payable	0
Gross capital formation		-50		
Net lending (+) / Net borrowing (-)		-76	**Net lending (+) / Net borrowing (-)**	76
Change in financial assets		30	Change in financial assets	76
Currency		10	Currency	
Loans		20	Loans	76
Change in financial liabilities		106	Change in financial liabilities	0
Currency		10	Currency	
Loans		96	Loans	0
Net lending (+) / Net borrowing (-)		-76	**Net lending (+) / Net borrowing (-)**	76
Opening balance sheet (at end of 1999)			**Opening balance sheet (at end of 1999)**	
Non-financial assets		1000		
Financial assets		300	Financial assets	150
Currency		200	Currency	
Loans		100	Loans	150
Financial liabilities		440	Financial liabilities	10
Currency		200	Currency	
Loans		240	Loans	10
Net worth		860	Net worth	140
Change in balance sheet			**Change in balance sheet**	
Non-financial assets		75		
Gross capital formation		50		
Consumption of fixed capital		-5		
Holding gain		30		
Financial assets		30	Financial assets	76
Financial liabilities		106	Financial liabilities	0
Change in net worth		-1	Change in net worth	76
Ending balance sheet (at end of 2000)			**Ending balance sheet (at end of 2000)**	
Non-financial assets		1075		
Financial assets		330	Financial assets	226
Financial liabilities		546	Financial liabilities	10
Net worth		859	Net worth	216
Change in net worth		-1	**Change in net worth**	76

PART II

INTEGRATED ACCOUNTS
BY INDUSTRIES
AND INSTITUTIONAL SECTORS

Chapter 9

Industry and sector breakdown

A. OBJECTIVES

9.1.   The breakdown of economic activities by industry aims to:

a) Study in detail costs of production of industries;
b) Use the cost details to forecast or estimate input requirement for production;
c) Develop the detailed supply and use tables as the basic tool to balance the supply and use of products by industries, and to link production accounts by industries to production accounts by institutional sectors in a systematic manner;
d) Compile ratios of value added over output of industries of the benchmark year (for which detailed census on output and cost is carried out) for use in estimating value added by industry and GDP for the non-benchmark years.

9.2.   The breakdown of the economic accounts of the nation into institutional sector units, such as corporations, government, non-profit institutions and households, aims to study their economic behaviour in terms of the kind of income they receive, how incomes are used, how gross capital formation is financed, how they manage their financial portfolio and what their net worth is.

9.3.   The present chapter will consider the statistical unit of industries and institutional sectors and types of institutional sectors.

B. WHAT IS AN INDUSTRY / ESTABLISHMENT?

9.4.   An industry is a grouping of establishments engaged in the same or similar kinds of activities classified in the same International Standard Industrial Classification of All Economic Activities (ISIC) code.

9.5.   An establishment is an enterprise or a part of it that is situated in a single location in which only a single productive activity accounts for most of its value added. In principle, an establishment may not decide on its financial matters; the latter is decided by the enterprise that owns the establishment. Thus, an establishment can only serve as the statistical unit for collecting production data on economic activities or industry.

9.6.   To be classified as an establishment in SNA, an establishment must produce output that is used by other establishments or other final consumers. Goods and services that are produced within the establishments for own intermediate uses are not counted as output.

9.7.   An enterprise which is an institutional unit (discussed below), may consist of many establishments classified into different ISIC codes.

FIGURE 9.1. RELATIONSHIP BETWEEN ESTABLISHMENT UNIT AND ENTERPRISE UNIT

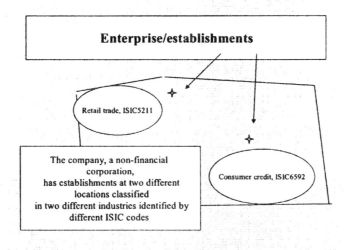

C. WHAT IS AN INSTITUTIONAL UNIT?

9.8.   An institutional unit is an economic entity that is capable, in its own right, of owning assets, incurring liabilities and engaging in economic activities with other entities. It takes economic decisions on what to produce and how to finance its activities and is directly accountable at law.

9.9.   Examples of an institutional unit are an enterprise, a household, a bank, a school, a church, a cooperative and an autonomous government unit.

9.10.   The resident institutional units make up the total economy.

D. ANCILLARY CORPORATIONS / ACTIVITIES

9.11.   If a subsidiary corporation, wholly owned by a parent corporation, provides strictly confined services to the parent company or its other subsidiaries, SNA treats it not as a separate institutional unit but an integral part of the parent company.

9.12.   Similarly, ancillary activities in a corporation providing strictly confined services (such as accounting, computing, personal management) to the establishments in the corporation are not treated as a separate establishment.

9.13   In principle, ancillary corporations / activities do not generate output.

E. INSTITUTIONAL SECTORS IN THE ECONOMY

9.14.   SNA recommends subdividing the economy into five mutually exclusive institutional sectors:

        a)   Non-financial corporations sector;
        b)   Financial corporations sector;
        c)   General government sector;

d) Households sector;

e) Non-profit institutions serving households (NPISHs) sector.

TABLE T9.1. CLASSIFICATION OF INSTITUTIONAL SECTORS IN SNA

Non-financial corporations	General government (alternative 1)
Public non-financial corporations	Central government
National private non-financial corporations	State government
Foreign-controlled non-financial corporations	Local government
Financial corporations	Social security funds
Central banks	Central government
Other depository corporations	State government
Deposit money corporations	Local government
Public	**General government (alternative 2)**
National private	Central government
Foreign controlled	Central government
Other deposit corporations except above	Central government social security funds
Public	State government
National private	State government
Foreign controlled	State government social security funds
Other financial intermediaries, except insurance corporations and pension funds	Local government
Public	Local government
National private	Local government social security funds
Foreign controlled	**Households**
Financial auxiliaries	Employers
Public	Own account workers
National private	Recipients of property and transfer income
Foreign controlled	Recipients of property income
Insurance corporations and pension funds	Recipients of pensions
Public	Recipients of other transfers
National private	**Non-profit institutions serving households**
Foreign controlled	**Rest of the world**

F. AN EXAMPLE OF THE NEED FOR BOTH INDUSTRY BREAKDOWN AND INSTITUTIONAL SECTORING

9.15.   Education services may be fully market oriented, free or almost free, or provided free or almost free and financed by the government, households or non-profit institutions (NPIs).

9.16.   To study the costs of operation and value added generated by education, all education establishments are classified into industry ISIC 92, producing education services.

9.17.   To study the role of the institutional sectors:

a) Market-oriented schools are classified into the non-financial corporations sector;

b) Government-funded schools are classified into the general government sector;

c) NPI-funded schools are classified into NPI serving households (NPISHs).

FIGURE F9.2. SECTORING BY INDUSTRY AND SECTOR: AN EXAMPLE

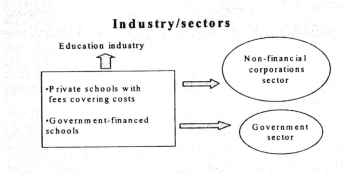

G. CORPORATIONS

9.18. A corporation is a legal entity recognized by laws of the nation independently of its shareholders. It is owned and controlled by private shareholders or by the Government. Control means the ability to determine corporate policies by appointing appropriate directors, if necessary.

NON-FINANCIAL CORPORATIONS SECTOR

9.19. The sector includes all resident corporations that are owned by private shareholders or the government and produce goods and non-financial services.

9.20. It may also include **quasi-corporations**, which are unincorporated but keep full business accounts. The shareowners of those quasi-corporations are legally and financially liable to the operation of the corporations. A quasi-corporation may be a sole proprietorship, partnership or even a government-owned production unit, with full business accounting.

FINANCIAL CORPORATIONS SECTOR

9.21. The sector includes all resident corporations that are owned by private shareholders or the government and produce financial services.

9.22. The financial corporations sector can be divided into the following sub-sectors:

a) The central bank;
b) Other depository corporations/banks;
c) Other financial intermediaries, such as investment banks, financial leasing companies, hire purchase companies and consumer credit companies;
d) Financial auxiliaries, such as securities brokers and loan or insurance brokers;
e) Insurance corporations and pension funds.

H. HOUSEHOLD SECTOR

9.23. A household is a small group of people who share the same living accommodation, pool some of their income, and consume certain type of goods and services collectively, mainly housing and food.

9.24. The sector includes resident household units as consumers and also all their economic activities that are unincorporated.

9.25. Unincorporated enterprises, which are owned by households but have complete business accounts, are classified as quasi-corporations in the corporations sector.

SUBDIVISION OF THE HOUSEHOLD SECTOR

9.26. The household sector may be subdivided by main sources of income into:

  a) Employers;
  b) Own-account workers;
  c) Employees;
  d) Recipients of property and transfer incomes.

I. NON-PROFIT INSTITUTIONS AND NON-PROFIT INSTITUTIONS SERVING HOUSEHOLDS

9.27. Non-profit institutions are legal or social entities created to provide goods and services to other institutional units, whose status does not permit them to create income, profit or financial gains for those who control and finance them.

9.28. NPISHs includes only NPIs that serve households and produce non-market goods and services without charges or whose prices are economically insignificant.

9.29. If NPIs are controlled or if 50 per cent of their costs are paid for by the corporations or general government sectors, they should be classified to those sectors respectively, not to the NPISHs sector.

J. GENERAL GOVERNMENT SECTOR

9.30. The general government sector includes legal entities which have legislative, judicial or executive authority over other institutional units.

9.31. It includes central government, state governments, local governments, social security funds and NPIs serving the government.

9.32. It produces mainly non-market services that are provided free or at economically insignificant prices. Services could be collective, such as defence, or individual, such as health and education.

K. WHAT SHOULD BE EXCLUDED FROM THE GENERAL GOVERNMENT SECTOR?

9.33. Government may control production by:

  a) Setting up public corporations;
  b) Creating NPIs and mainly or entirely financing them;
  c) Producing market goods and services without setting up separate legal units but having full business accounts - called quasi-corporations.

9.34.   As long as those entities can charge market prices or prices that cover over 50 percent of costs, they are excluded from the government sector.

EXERCISES ON ACCOUNTS OF THE GOVERNMENT SECTOR

Given the following government financial statistics (A), prepare:

1. Output, intermediate consumption, final consumption expenditures of government, individual and collective consumption expenditures of government, gross capital formation, primary incomes, current transfers.
2. Production, income and capital accounts of the government sector, using form B.

A. **Government expenditures and revenues**

1. Revenue		**187**
Sales to households		5
Sales to corporations		10
Taxes		150
Other taxes on production	15	
Taxes on income	135	
Interest income		12
International assistance		10
<div align="center">**2. Expense**</div>		**167**
Uses of goods and services		
Collective non-market activities	80	
Goods and services	20	
Compensation of employees	58	
Consumption of fixed capital	2	
Individual non-market activities	20	
Goods and services	5	
Compensation of employees	14	
Consumption of fixed capital	1	
Social benefits in kind (reimbursements included)[a]		20
Social benefits in cash		22
Interest payment		10
Capital transfers		10
International assistance		5
3. Net operating balance (1)- (2)		**20**
Consumption of fixed capital		3
Collective non-market activities	2	
Collective non-market activities	1	
4. Gross operating balance (Net operating balance plus consumption of fixed capital)		**23**
5. Acquisition less disposal of non financial assets [b]		**30**
Purchases less disposal of capital goods	20	
Own-construction	7	
Major repairs	3	
6. Net lending/net borrowing (4) – (5)		**-7**
Sale of government bonds		7

[a] Including government purchases of goods and services to be distributed free to households and reimbursement for households' expenditures on goods and services.

[b] The IMF's *Government Finance Statistics Manual* uses net operating balance and net acquisition less disposal of non-financial assets where consumption of fixed capital is net out.

B. Accounts of government

	Uses	Resources
Output Intermediate consumption **Gross value added**		
Gross value added Taxes less subsidies on products **Gross operating surplus**		
Gross operating surplus Property income receivable Property income payable **Gross national income**		
Gross national income Current transfer receivable Current transfer payable **Gross disposable income**		
Gross disposable income Final consumption **Gross saving**		
Gross saving Capital transfer receivable Capital transfer payable Gross capital formation		
Net lending (+) / net borrowing		

Notes to form B

- "Uses", which is on the left side of the accounts, relates to transactions that reduce the amount of economic value of a unit or sector.
- "Resources", which is on the right side of the accounts, relates to transactions that increase the amount of economic value of a unit or sector.
- Intermediate consumption and other types of transactions in the government outlays can be classified as indicated in form C below in order to facilitate the derivation of output, intermediate consumption, value added and final consumption of the government sector according to functions. Market output which is sales and/or fees charged for government services are taken from government revenues. Similarly own-account capital formation is not for final consumption expenditure.
- 01 to 10 are codes classifying transaction outlays by for government functions: 01 (General public service), 02 (Defence), 03 (Public order and safety), 04 (Economic affairs), 05 (Environmental protection), 06 (Housing and community amenities), 07 (Health), 08 (Recreation, culture and religion), 09 (Education) and 10 (Social protection). For more detailed classification and instructions, see *Classifications of Expenditure According to Purpose (United Nations publication, Sales No. E.00.XVII.6).*

C. Classifications of government outlays according to functions

	Output	Intermediate consumption	Compensation of employees	Consumption of fixed capital	Market output	Social benefits in kind	Final consumption	Own-account capital formation	Gross capital formation	Subsidies	Property income	Social benefits other than in kind	Other current transfers	Capital transfers	Securities other than shares	Loans	Shares and other equity
	(1) = (2)+(3)+(4)+(8)	(2)	(3)	(4)	(5)	(6)	(7)= (1)- (8)- (5)+(6)	(8)	(9)	(10)	(11)	(12)	(13)	(14)	(15)	(16)	(17)
01	General public services																
02	Defense																
...																	
10	Social protection																

SOLUTIONS

SOLUTION TO QUESTION 1

Output =	Current expenditures on goods and services to produce government services + Own major repairs + Own-construction + Compensation of employees + Consumption of fixed capital = 25 + 3 + 7 + 72 + 3 = 110
Intermediate consumption =	Expenditures for own major repairs and own construction + Current expenditures on goods and services = 10 + 25 = 35
Final consumption expenditure =	Output - (own major repairs - own construction) - Sales to households and corporations + Social benefits in kind = 110 - (3+7) - (5+10) + 20 = 105
Individual final consumption expenditure =	Individual non-market output + Social benefits in kind - Sales = 20 + 20 -15 = 25
Collective final consumption expenditure =	Current expenditure on collective output = 80
Gross capital formation =	Government capital expenditures = 30
Current transfers payable =	Social benefits in cash + International assistance = 22 + 5 = 27

SOLUTION TO QUESTION 2
Production, income and capital accounts

C. Accounts of the government sector	Uses	Resources
Output at basic prices		110
Less Intermediate consumption	35	
Gross value added at basic prices	75	
Gross value added at basic prices		75
Less Compensation of employees	72	
Less Other taxes on production	0	
Gross operating surplus	3	
Gross operating surplus		3
Plus Property income receivable		12
Less Property income payable	10	
Gross national income	5	
Gross national income		5
Plus Current transfer receivable		160
Less Current transfer payable	27	
Gross disposable income	138	
Gross disposable income		138
Less Final consumption	105	
Gross saving	33	
Gross saving		33
Plus Capital transfer receivable		
Less Capital transfer payable		-10
Less Gross capital formation	30	
Net lending (+) / Net borrowing (-)	7	

Chapter 10

Supply and use tables:
integration of industries, products and institutional sectors

A. OBJECTIVES OF SUPPLY AND USE TABLES

10.1.   Supply and use tables are tools used to check the consistency of statistics on flows of goods and services on the principle that the total supply of each product is equal to its total uses.

10.2.   They are used to derive value added and final demand (final consumption expenditure, gross capital formation, exports and imports) in current and constant prices in a very detailed, integrated and consistent manner.

10.3.   Value added / output ratios by industries can be used to quickly derive annual and quarterly estimates of value added and thus GDP.

10.4.   Supply and use tables are also used to derive the input-output table for the purpose of economic impact analysis and forecasting.

10.5.   SNA requires only the cross-classification of gross value added by industries and institutional sectors. The presentation in the present chapter shows the full cross-classification of output, intermediate consumption and gross value added by industries and institutional sectors for the sake of exposition only.

B. ORGANIZATION OF SUPPLY AND USE TABLES

10.6   The supply table (table T10.1) shows, along each row, the kind of product produced by domestic industries and supplied by the rest of the world. They are either in basic prices or c.i.f. Total supply of each product in purchasers' prices is obtained by adding in trade and transport margins, and taxes less subsidies on products. C.i.f./f.o.b. adjustment is for obtaining total imports in f.o.b. Down each industry column are products produced by an industry. In the example provided, industry 2 produces 10 of product 1 and 200 of product 2.

10.6.   The use table (table T10.2) shows, down each industry column, the uses of goods and services (i.e., the cost structure) of industries and the value added generated by them. Along each row of the same table are the uses of each product. They are all in purchasers' prices. The negative entry in the trade and transport column is to make the total of row 2 in the supply table equivalent to the total of row 2 in the use table, which shows only product 2 directly used by industries (not margins).

10.7.   Industries may be classified by the International Standard Industrial Classification of All Economic Activities. Products (goods and services) are classified by the Central Product

Classification. For the most aggregated level of those United Nations classification systems, see table T10.3.

TABLE T10.1. THE SUPPLY TABLE: OUTPUTS AT BASIC PRICES

	Industry 1	Industry 2	Imports c.i.f. (Total f.o.b.)	C.i.f./f.o.b. adjustment[a]	Trade and transport margins	Taxes less subsidies on products	Total supply at purchasers' prices
Product 1	100	10	25		10	5	150
Product 2	0	200	10	-2	-10	10	208
C.i.f./f.o.b. adjustment[a]			-2				
Output/Total	100	210	33		0	15	358

[a]C.i.f./f.o.b. adjustment is for changing imports c.i.f. values into f.o.b. values See also table T6.1; the value to be deducted is the freight and insurance on imported goods.

TABLE T10.2. THE USE TABLE: USES AT PURCHASERS' PRICES

	Industry 1	Industry 2	Export	Final consumption expenditure	Gross capital formation	Total uses at purchasers' prices
Product 1	10	40	30	50	20	150
Product 2	30	70	40	68		208
Value added	60	100				
Output/Total	100	210	70	118	20	358

GDP = value added + taxes less subsidies on products = 160 + 15 = 175	GDP = final consumption + gross capital formation + Exports – imports = 118 + 20 + 70 - 33 = 175

C. BALANCING SUPPLY AND USE TABLE

10.8. The total supply and the total use at purchasers' prices of each product in SUT must be equal to each other. Those values are, however, statistically constructed. They are not data that can be collected through surveys. Data collected by censuses or surveys include output at basic prices, imports c.i.f., taxes less subsidies on products, trade and transport margins on traded goods, exports, final consumption expenditure and gross capital formation.

10.9. To statistically create the total supply at purchasers' prices of each good, data on goods produced by industries must be supplemented by data on import, wholesale and retail trade and transport margins on the same good which are collected by censuses or surveys, and by taxes less subsidies on margins which are estimated based on tax rates and the tax information from the government budget data. Trade margins on each good are calculated when the output of trade is calculated. Transport margins classified by CPC are the output of the good-carrying transport services less the transport of goods directly paid by purchasers.

10.10. The total supply at purchasers' prices may initially serve as a total control for the total use at purchasers' prices in the use table for every product. However in balancing the total supply and the total use of every product, one may have to modify the total supply if the total use is shown to be more reliable. Uses of each product for intermediate consumption are normally estimated by the gross outputs of industries which use that product as intermediate consumption and the input ratios obtained through limited surveys on intermediate consumption by industries. Data on the government final consumption are obtained from administrative records. Gross capital formation is obtained as a result of reconciling data on gross capital formation obtained by survey on gross capital formation, data on gross industry outputs and imports that can be classified as capital goods. Household final consumption is normally obtained as a balancing item, but it should be verified by data obtained from surveys of household expenditure and/or of retail sales.

TABLE 10.3. INTERNATIONAL CLASSIFICATION OF ECONOMIC ACTIVITES AND PRODUCTS AT THE MOST AGGREGATED LEVEL

International Standard Classification of All Economic Activities, Revision 3 (ISIC, Rev. 3)	Central Product Classification, Version 1.0 (CPC, Version 1.0)
Agriculture, hunting and forestry	Agriculture, forestry and fishery products
Fishing	
Mining and quarrying	Ores and minerals; electricity, gas and water
Manufacturing	Food products, beverages and tobacco; textiles, apparel and leather products
Electricity, gas and water supply	Other transportable goods, except metal products, machinery and equipment
Construction	Metals products, machinery and equipment
Wholesale and retail trade; repair of motor vehicles and personal and household goods	Construction work and constructions
Hotels and restaurants	Trade services; hotel and restaurant services
Transport, storage and communications	Transport, storage and communications services
Financial intermediation	Business services; agricultural, mining and manufacturing services
Real estate, renting and business activities	Community, social and personal services
Public administration and defense; compulsory security	
Education	
Health and social work	
Other community, social and personal activities	
Private households with employed persons	
Extra-territorial organizations and bodies	

D. BREAKDOWN OF FINAL USES

10.11. Final consumption expenditure and gross capital formation in the use table should be subdivided into separate expenditures for:

    a) The household sector;
    b) The general government sector;
    c) The non-profit institutions serving households sector.

Final consumption expenditure of households records all the goods and services bought by the household sector.

10.12. Final consumption expenditure of the government sector records:

    a) The output of government that is not sold (30 in the example);
    b) The purchase of goods and services by government to be distributed free to households or the purchases by households to be reimbursed by the government (8 in the example provided). Those goods and services are called **social benefits in kind**.

TABLE T10.4. BREAKDOWN OF FINAL USES IN THE USE TABLE

	Final consumption expenditure		Gross capital formation		
	Households & NPISHs	Government	Households & NPISHs	Government	Corporations
Product 1	30	8	8	2	10
Product 2	50	30			
Total	80	38	8	2	10

E. BREAKDOWN OF VALUE ADDED

10.13.   In the economy, each sector may engage in a variety of economic activities. Establishments may therefore be identified by the sector to which they belong.

10.14.   In so doing, value added by each sector may be obtained, which is important for deriving and cross-classifying output, intermediate consumption and value added by industries and sectors.

TABLE T10.5. BREAKDOWN OF VALUE ADDED

	Corporations		Households & NPISHs		Government	
	Industry 1	Industry 2	Industry 1	Industry 2	Industry 1	Industry 2
Product 1	5	30	5	8		2
Product 2	15	54	15	12		4
Value added	30	68	30	20		12
Output	50	152	50	40		18
Value added by corporations: 30 + 68 = 98 Value added by households and NPISHs: 30 +20 = 50 Value added by government: 12						

F. DATA REQUIREMENT FOR SECTORIZATION OF PRODUCTION

10.15.   The same set of data collected by surveys of establishments can be used for both industry and sectoral production analysis.

10.16.   Establishment data to be used for both purposes requires that each establishment be identified by institutional origin, as follows:

	Establishment data for financial and non-financial corporations	Establishment data for unincorporated private enterprises (households)	Production data by products or activities (applicable to agricultural, fishing and forestry products)	General government	NPISHs
Type of data	Surveys and business accounts	Surveys	Land use and yield surveys and others and surveys on production costs	Administrative records	Surveys and business accounts

EXERCISE ON SETTING UP THE USE AND SUPPLY TABLES

Set up the use and supply tables with the information below. Derive the unknown data by balancing the total use and the total supply of each product. In the exercise, product 1 is a good and product 2 is a service. Calculate GDP by production approach and final expenditure approach.

Information:

Output at basic prices of industry 1:
        Product 1:   150;   Product 2:   30
Output at basic prices of industry 2:
        Product 1:   0;   Product 2:   100
Inputs at purchasers' prices to industry 1:
        Product 1:   40;   Product 2:   30
Inputs at purchasers' prices to industry 2:
        Product 1:   10;   Product 2:   20
Imports c.i.f:
        Product 1:   40;   Product 2:   20
Insurance and freight on imported goods: 3
Exports f.o.b.:
        Product 1:   50;   Product 2:   15
Gross capital formation at purchasers' prices:
        Product 1:   50;   Product 2:   7
Trade and transport margins:
        Product 1:   70
Taxes less subsidies on products:
        Product 1:   20;   Product 2:   10

Note: use the following framework for the exercise:

The supply table

	Industry 1	Industry 2	Imports c.i.f. (Total f.o.b.)	C.i.f./f.o.b. adjustment	Trade and transport margins	Taxes less subsidies on products	Total supply at purchasers' prices
Product 1							
Product 2							
C.i.f./f.o.b. adjustment							
Output/Total							

The use table

	Industry 1	Industry 2	Exports		Final consumption expenditure	Gross capital formation	Total uses at purchasers' prices
Product 1							
Product 2							
Value added							
Output/Total							

88

SOLUTIONS

The supply table

	Industry 1	Industry 2	Imports c.i.f. (Total f.o.b.)	C.i.f./f.o.b. adjustment	Trade and transport margins	Taxes less subsidies on products	Total supply at purchasers' prices
Product 1	150	0	40		70	20	280
Product 2	30	100	20	-3	-70	10	87
C.i.f./f.o.b. adjustment			-3				
Output/Total	180	100	57	-3	0	30	

The use table

	Industry 1	Industry 2	Exports		Final consumption expenditure	Gross capital formation	Total uses at purchasers' prices
Product 1	40	10	50		130	50	280
Product 2	30	20	15		15	7	87
Value added	110	70					
Output/Total	180	100	65		145	57	

GDP by production approach: 110+70+30=210.
GDP by final expenditure approach: 65+145+57-57=210.

Chapter 11:

Institutional sector accounts

A. OBJECTIVES

11.1. Institutional sector accounts (or sector accounts) derive for each (institutional) sector value added, primary income, disposable income, final consumption expenditure, saving, gross capital formation, net lending (+) or net borrowing (-) like those of the whole economy.

11.2. Sector accounts provide information on transactions in income and financial flows between domestic sectors and between the domestic sectors and the rest of the world.

11.3. This information allows for an analysis of the institutional structure and behaviour of every institutional sector in the economy.

B. TYPES OF INCOME

11.4. Similar to the whole economy, each sector has the following types of income:

a) Primary income (compensation of employees, other taxes less subsidies on production, and property income);
b) Entrepreneurial income;
c) Disposable income.

11.5. The sum of incomes of all domestic sectors makes up the total for the whole economy.

11.6. The sum of all sectoral balances of primary income is gross national income (GNI).

C. SECTORAL BALANCE OF PRIMARY INCOME

11.7. Balance of primary income is equal to value added + primary income receivable - primary income payable.

11.8. Each item in the use side may be broken down into who the primary income is paid to and each item in the resource side may be broken down into who the primary income is received from (that possibility is applicable to subsequent accounts and so will not be restated.)

11.9. For the whole economy, only primary income from and to the rest of the world counts since payments and receipts between domestic sectors cancel each other out.

Uses		Resources	
		Value added	20
Primary income payable	5	Primary income receivable	10
Balance of primary income	25		

D. SECTORAL ENTREPRENEURIAL INCOME

11.10.   Entrepreneurial income is an approximation of net income (or profit) of the corporations sectors before dividends are distributed to shareholders.

11.11.   It is equal to value added + primary income receivable - primary income payable except dividends paid out to shareholders (or withdrawals by owners in the case of quasi-corporations).

11.12.   The concept of entrepreneurial income is useful only for the corporations sectors.

Uses		Resources	
		Value added	20
Primary income payable except dividends	1	Primary income receivable	10
Entrepreneurial income	29		

E. SECTORAL DISPOSABLE INCOME

11.13.   Disposable income is equal to balance of primary income + current transfers receivable - current transfers payable.

11.14.   For the whole economy, only current transfers from or to the rest of the world counts since payments and receipts between domestic sectors cancel each other out.

Uses		Resources	
		Balance of primary income	25
Current transfers payable	6	Current transfers receivable	5
Disposable income	24		

F. SECTORAL GROSS SAVING

11.15.   Gross saving is equal to disposable income - final consumption expenditure.

11.16.   Final consumption expenditure of the corporations sector is by definition zero.

11.17.   Sectoral gross saving may be positive or negative.

Uses		Resources	
		Disposable income	24
Final consumption expenditure	30		
Gross saving	-6		

G. SECTORAL NET LENDING (+) / NET BORROWING (-)

11.18. Net lending (+) or net borrowing (-) is equal to gross saving + net capital transfers - gross capital formation - net acquisition of non-produced non-financial assets.

11.19. For the whole economy, net acquisition of tangible non-produced assets must be zero, except for patented entities (see exception rule under figure F4.1).

Uses		Resources	
		Gross saving	-6
Gross capital formation	40	Net capital transfers	6
Net acquisition of non-produced, non-financial assets	10	• Capital transfers receivable	8
		• Capital transfers payable	-2
Net lending (+)/Net borrowing (-)	-50		

H. SECTORAL FINANCIAL ACCOUNTS

11.20. As for to the financial account of the nation, sectoral financial accounts have financial assets on the left side and financial liabilities on the right side. Net lending (+) / net borrowing (-) is equal to the total financial assets less the total liabilities. The net lending/net borrowing from the financial account must be equal to that of the capital account for each sector.

11.21. Each transaction in the financial account of a sector must have a counterpart in the financial account of another sector, except for monetary gold and SDRs issued by the International Monetary Fund (see paras. 5.4-5.10 above). In such a case, the asset of one sector is the liability of another sector. The breakdown of assets by the sectors that are liable and of liabilities by the sectors that hold them as assets provides the flow of funds. The flow of funds allows for the identification of flows of funds between sectors of the economy and the rest of the world. The flow of funds is important for understanding the mobilization of funds and the financial liabilities that the sectors incur to achieve it. For example, it is possible from the flow of funds to understand what types of liabilities the government uses to finance its deficit and which sectors it provides with financing.

Assets		Liabilities	
Net lending (+)/Net borrowing (-)	-50		
Total change in assets	100	Total change in liabilities	150
Monetary gold and SDRs		Monetary gold and SDRs	
Currency and deposits		Currency and deposits	
Securities other shares		Securities other shares	
Loans		Loans	
Shares and other equity		Shares and other equity	
Other accounts receivable		Other accounts payable	

I. SECTORAL BALANCE SHEETS

11.22. For institutional sector accounts balance sheets, see chapter 7 above.

Chapter 12

Other important issues in sector accounts

12.1. The present chapter will discuss two important issues relating to sector accounts:

    a) Final consumption expenditure versus actual final consumption;

    b) Business accounts versus national accounts.

A. FINAL CONSUMPTION EXPENDITURE VERSUS ACTUAL FINAL CONSUMPTION

1. OBJECTIVES

12.2. The main objective is to measure the consumption of households, not only from their own final expenditure but also from the expenditure of other sectors to benefit them.

12.3. **Final consumption expenditure** consists of expenditure incurred by residents on final goods and services (goods and services that are not used for the purpose of production).

12.4. **Actual final consumption** measures final goods and services *consumed* by the sectors through the expenditure incurred by the sectors themselves or **social transfers in kind** received from other sectors. Though actual final consumption is defined for all sectors, it is meaningful for analysis only for the household sector.

2. ACTUAL FINAL CONSUMPTION OF HOUSEHOLDS

12.5. Actual final consumption of households comes from three sources: their own final expenditure, the final expenditure of the government and that of non-profit institutions serving households. Thus, it is equal to the sum of:

    a) Final consumption expenditure of households;

    b) Social transfers in kind from the government;

    c) Social transfers in kind from non-profit institutions serving households (NPISHs).

12.6. The objective of the concept of the actual final consumption of households is to compare final consumption of households across space and time in the country and internationally, taking into account social policies of governments and activities of NPISHs.

Social transfers in kind

12.7. Social transfers in kind include:

    a) **Individual final expenditure of the government sector less sales**. This includes the output of individual goods and services which are produced by the government sector and distributed free to individuals, such as education, health, social security and welfare, sports and recreation, culture, provision of housing, collection of household refuse and operation of transport. It excludes general administration and regulatory and research expenditures in each category.

b) **Social benefits in kind**, which include (see also T.3.1):

i) Reimbursements from government's social security funds to households on specified goods and services bought by households on the market;

ii) Other social security benefits in kind except reimbursement. This includes goods and services which are *not produced* by the government sector but bought and distributed free or almost free to households under the social security funds (any payment by household must be deducted);

iii) Social assistance benefits in kind. This includes goods and services similar to *other social security benefits* but not under social security schemes.

FIGURE F12.1. RELATIONSHIP BETWEEN FINAL CONSUMPTION EXPENDITURE AND ACTUAL FINAL CONSUMPTION OF HOUSEHOLDS

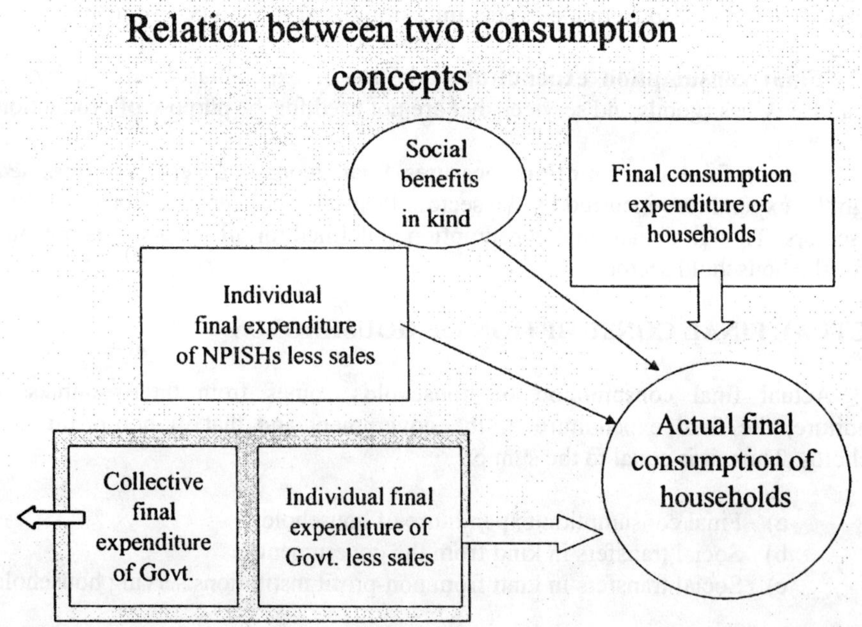

Relation between two consumption concepts

3. FINAL CONSUMPTION EXPENDITURE OF GENERAL GOVERNMENT

12.8. Government final consumption expenditure includes two parts:

a) **Output of government services less sales**. This output can be divided into two parts:

i) **Individual final consumption expenditure of government less sales**. This is the output of individual goods and services which are produced by the government sector and distributed free to individuals, such as education, health, social security and welfare, sports and recreation, culture, provision of housing, collection of household refuse and operation of transport. It excludes general administration and regulatory and research expenditures in each category. This part of the output of government goods and services less sales benefits directly individuals. It is part of the **social transfers in kind** previously discussed;

ii) **Collective final consumption expenditure of government**: This is equal to the non-market government output (not for sale) less individual final consumption expenditure of government;

b) **Social benefits in kind**: see definition in paragraph 12.7(b) above.

FIGURE F12.2. COMPONENTS OF GOVERNMENT FINAL CONSUMPTION EXPENDITURE

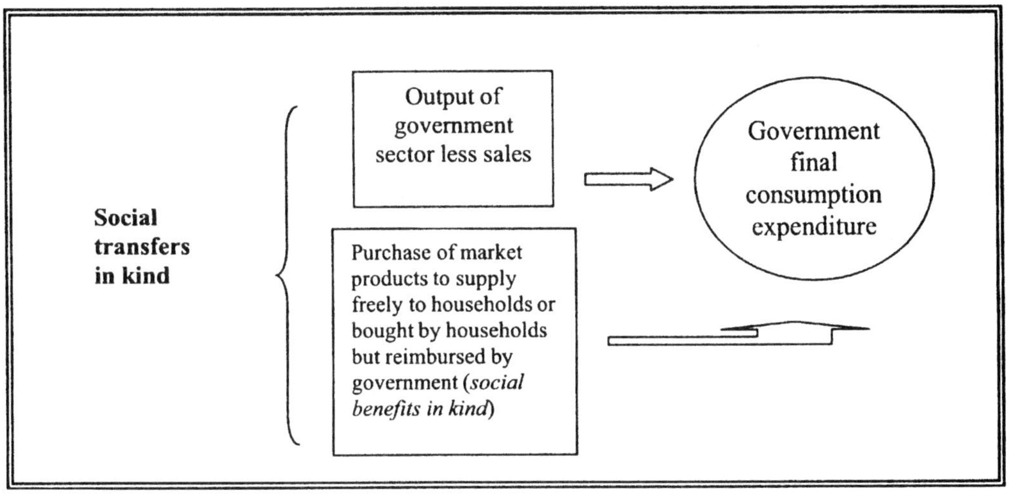

4. FINAL CONSUMPTION EXPENDITURE OF NPISHs

12.9.   Except for the part sold, final consumption expenditure of NPISHs is considered individual final consumption, i.e., all of it directly benefits individuals. Individual final consumption of NPISHs is also called transfers of individual non-market goods and services from NPISHs.

5. CLASSIFICATION OF CONSUMPTION EXPENDITURE

12.10.   There are three international classification schemes of expenditure according to purposes that help to aggregate final consumption expenditure and actual final consumption for comparison purposes:

a) The Classification of the Functions of Government (COFOG);
b) The Classification of Individual Consumption According to Purpose (COICOP);
c) The Classification of the Purposes of Non-Profit Institutions Serving Households (COPNI).

12.11   The main classes of consumption by purposes include:

a) Food and non-alcoholic beverages;

b)   Alcoholic beverages, tobacco and narcotics;
c)   Clothing and footwear;
d)   Housing, water, electricity, gas and other fuels;
e)   Furnishings, household equipment and routine household maintenance;
f)   Health;
g)   Transport;
h)   Communication;
i)   Recreation and culture;
j)   Education;
k)   Restaurant and hotels;
l)   Miscellaneous goods and services;
m) Individual consumption of non-profits institutions serving households;
  i)   Housing;
  ii)   Health;
  iii)   Recreation and culture;
  iv)   Education;
  v)   Social protection;
  vi)   Other services;
n) Individual consumption expenditure of general government:
  i)   Housing;
  ii)   Health;
  iii)   Recreation and culture;
  iv)   Education;
  v)   Social protection.

12.12.   The classifications mentioned above are published in *Classifications of Expenditure According to Purpose* (United Nations publication, Sales No. 00.XVII.6).

B. BUSINESS ACCOUNTS VERSUS NATIONAL ACCOUNTS

1. OBJECTIVES

12.13. Business accounts provide information on the financial situation of corporations. The conceptual similarities and differences between business accounts and national accounts need to be known by national account statisticians so that the information can be used properly.

2. SIMILARITIES BETWEEN BUSINESS ACCOUNTS AND NATIONAL ACCOUNTS

12.14. Business accounts and national accounts record transactions on an accrual basis (as opposed to cash basis). Payments, which are supposed to be paid, are recorded as payables; the part of payment not yet paid is also recorded as a liability (i.e., accounts payable) in the financial accounts and balance sheets. Receipts, which are supposed to be received, are recorded as receivables; the part not yet received is also recorded as an asset in the financial accounts and balance sheets.12.15.   The two systems have more or less the same kind of sequence of accounts but different names. Thus:

National accounts	Business accounts
Production accounts and various income accounts	Profit and loss statement
Capital account	
Financial account	Change in the financial position and cash flow statement
Capital account, balance sheet	Balance sheet

3. DIFFERENCES BETWEEN BUSINESS ACCOUNTS AND NATIONAL ACCOUNTS

12.16.   The differences between business accounts and national accounts are as follows:

National accounts	Business accounts
Record output, intermediate consumption and value added.	Record sales and cost of sales.
Value inventories, consumption of fixed capital and assets at market prices.	Value inventories, consumption of fixed capital and assets at historic prices or book values.
Capital gains or loss are not recorded as income or cost but changes in the balance sheet due to changes in prices (revaluation account)	Realized capital gains or loss are recorded in the profit and loss statement as income or cost.
Only costs actually incurred are recorded.	Cost allowances (assumed based on past behavior) such as bad debt allowance are recorded.

4. USES OF BUSINESS ACCOUNTS IN NATIONAL ACCOUNTS

12.17.   Business accounts can be used to prepare the full sequence of accounts of the corporations sectors, but with necessary adjustments.

12.18.   The handbook *Links between Business Accounting and National Accounting* (United Nations publication, Sales No. 00.XVII.13) provides detailed guidelines to link and adjust business accounts to national accounts.

5. AN EXAMPLE TO CONTRAST OR CONVERT BUSINESS ACCOUNTS AND NATIONAL ACCOUNTS

12.19.   In table T12.1, that a value of 100 is manufactured but not yet sold in the accounting period.

12.20.   Output can be calculated as the sum of production cost or as sales less change in inventory. Thus:

production cost = cost of raw materials and services + labour + consumption of fixed capital = 100;

sale + changes in inventory = 0 + 100

However, this is only an approximation. If output in terms of quantity is known, output must be calculated as the product of quantity and unit basic price (or equivalent market price). Consumption of fixed capital and depreciation is assumed to be zero here. Otherwise, depreciation must be introduced as part of cost of sales in business accounts and consumption of fixed capital must be calculated and included as part of the production cost when deriving national account output. Consumption of fixed capital is not the same as depreciation. For an explanation of how to calculate consumption of fixed capital, see *Links between Business Accounting and National Accounting* (United Nations publication, Sales No. 00.XVII.13), para. 2.22 and chap. 8.

TABLE T12.1. PRODUCTION AND INCOME ACCOUNTS: AN EXAMPLE OF CONVERSION

National accounts		Business accounts	
Output at basic prices		Sales	0
Equal production cost	100	- Cost of sales/manufactured	0
- Intermediate consumption at purchasers' prices	50	Equal Opening inventory 0	
= Value added	50	plus Cost of raw materials/services 50	
- Labour cost	50	plus Labour cost 50	
= Operating surplus	0	less Closing inventory 100	
		= Gross profit	0
+ Net interest	5	+ Net interest	5
- Gross capital formation (=inventory)	100	= Net income	5
= Net borrowing	-95		

TABLE T12.2. BALANCE SHEETS: AN EXAMPLE OF CONVERSION

National accounts		Business accounts	
Change in assets		Change in assets	
Change in inventory	100	Change in inventory	100
Change in liabilities		Change in liabilities	
Loan	95	Loan	95
Equity	5	Retained earnings	5

EXERCISES ON LINKING BUSINESS ACCOUNTS TO NATIONAL ACCOUNTS

Use the following business accounts (A and B) of a corporation to:

1. Compute output, intermediate consumption, compensation of employees, property income receivable, property income payable, current transfer payable, gross capital formation.
2. Fill out the attached form of the sequence accounts (C).

A. Profit and loss statement of a manufacturer, 31 December 1991

+	Sales net of returns and sale taxes			150
-	Cost of goods sold			-90
	Cost of goods bought for resale		-10	
	Cost of manufactured goods sold	80	-80	
	Opening inventory of finished and semi-finished goods	10		
	Cost of manufacturing	85		
	Materials and services used	30		
	Compensation of employees	50		
	Depreciation	5		
	Closing inventory of finished and semi-finished goods	-15		
=	Gross profit			60
-	Operating expenses			-32
	Materials and services used		-10	
	Compensation of employees		-20	
	Depreciation		-2	
=	Operating income			28
+	Interest income			2
+	Dividends received			2
-	Interest expenses			-10
=	Net income before taxes			22
-	Business income taxes			-3
=	Net income after taxes			19
-	Dividends paid			-1
=	Retained earnings			18

B. Balance sheets

	31-Dec-91	31-Dec-90
Assets		
Cash	45	20
Shares	20	20
Inventories	20	25
Finished and semi-finished goods	15	10
Materials and supplies	5	15
Fixed assets	43	45
Fixed assets at cost	55	50
Accumulated depreciation	-12	-5
Total	128	110
Liabilities and shareowners' equity		
Total liabilities		
Loans	65	65
Shareowners' equity	63	45
Shareowners' contribution	45	45
Retained earnings	18	0
Total	128	110

Notes:

- To complete the exercise:

  o One should assume that consumption of fixed capital is the same as depreciation. In actual work, consumption of fixed capital should be computed as part of the work to compile capital stocks.

  o Service charges for financial intermediation are assumed to be non-existent. In actual work, service charges for financial intermediation (FISIM) must be computed and treated as part of intermediate consumption. They are part of interest payments and receipts.

  o Prices are assumed to be constant during the two periods so that there is no need to revalue fixed assets and change in inventories. Thus there is no holding gain or loss.

- The measurement of capital stocks and consumption of fixed capital and the adjustment for financial intermediation service charges are discussed in paras. 2.92-2.99 above; for more details, see *Links between Business Accounts and National Accounts* (United Nations publication, Sales No. 00.XVII.13).

C. Accounts of corporations sectors

	Uses	Resources
Output at basic prices		
Intermediate consumption at purchasers' prices		
Gross value added		
Compensation of employees		
Other taxes on production		
Gross operating surplus		
Property income receivable		
Property income payable		
Gross income		
Current transfer receivable		
Current transfer payable		
Gross disposable income		
Final consumption		
Gross saving		
Capital transfer receivable		
Capital transfer payable		
Gross capital formation		
Net lending (+) / net borrowing		
Change in financial assets		
Currency		
Loans		
Change in financial liabilities		
Currency		
Loans		
Net lending (+) / net borrowing		
Opening balance sheet		
Non-financial assets		
Financial assets		
Currency		
Loans		
Financial liabilities		
Currency		
Loans		
Net worth		
Change in balance sheet		
Non-financial assets		
Gross capital formation		
Consumption of fixed capital		
Holding gain		
Financial assets		
Financial liabilities		
Change in net worth		
Ending balance sheet		
Non-financial assets		
Financial assets		
Financial liabilities		
Net worth		
Change in net worth		

SOLUTIONS

SOLUTION TO QUESTION 1

Output at basic prices =	Sales - Goods bought for resale + Change in inventory of finished and semi-finished goods = 150 - 10 + (15 -10) = 145
Intermediate consumption at purchasers' prices =	Materials and services used = 40
Compensation of employees =	50 + 20 = 70
Property income receivable =	Interest receivable + dividends receivable = 2 + 2 = 4
Property income payable =	Interest expenses + dividends payable = 10 + 1 = 11
Current transfer payable =	Business income taxes = 3
Gross capital formation =	Change in fixed assets at cost + Change in inventory (55 -50) + (20 -25) = 0

SOLUTION TO QUESTION 2

Production, income and capital accounts

C. Accounts of corporations sectors		
	Uses	Resources
Output at basic prices		145
Less Intermediate consumption at purchasers' prices	40	
Gross value added at basic prices	105	
Gross value added at basic prices		105
Less Compensation of employees	70	
Less Other taxes on production	0	
Gross operating surplus	35	
Gross operating surplus		35
Plus Property income receivable		4
Less Property income payable	11	
Gross income	28	
Gross income		28
Plus Current transfer receivable		0
Less Current transfer payable	3	
Gross disposable income	25	
Gross disposable income		25
Less Final consumption	0	
Gross saving	25	
Gross saving		25
Plus Capital transfer receivable		0
Less Capital transfer payable		0
Less Gross capital formation	0	
Net lending (+) / Net borrowing (-)		25

Financial accounts

	Assets	Liabilities
1. **Change in financial assets**	**25**	
Currency	25	
Loans		
Shares and other equity	0	
2. **Change in financial liabilities**		**0**
Currency		
Loans		0
Shares and other equity		0
Net lending (+) / Net borrowing (1-2)		**25**

Balance sheets

Opening balance sheet	Assets	Liabilities
1. Non-financial assets	**70**	
Fixed assets at cost less consumption of fixed capital	45	
Inventories	25	
2. Financial assets	**40**	
Currency	20	
Loans	0	
Shares and equity	20	
3. Financial liabilities		**65**
Currency		0
Loans		65
4. Net worth (1+2-6)		**45**
Change in balance sheet		
5. Non-financial assets		**-7**
Gross capital formation		0
Consumption of fixed capital		-7
Holding gain/loss		0
6. Financial assets	**25**	
Cash	25	
7. Financial liabilities		**0**
8. Change in net worth (5+6-7)		**18**
Ending balance sheet		
9. Non-financial assets	**63**	
Fixed assets at cost less consumption of fixed capital	43	
Inventories	20	
Holding gain/loss	0	
10. Financial assets	**65**	
Currency	45	
Loans	0	
Shares and equity	20	
11. Financial liabilities		**65**
Currency		0
Loans		65
12. Net worth (9+10-11)		**63**
Change in net worth (12-4)		**18**

Chapter 13

Price and volume measures in national accounts

A. OBJECTIVES

13.1.   GDP and its components at different time periods must be valued at the constant prices of a certain base year for the purpose of calculating real rates of growth.

13.2.   The present chapter aims to explain how to derive GDP and its components in constant prices, which are also called the volume measure of GDP[10] and its components.

13.3.   It first explains the types of price indexes that are widely collected, and then the different types of volume indexes resulting from aggregating different quantities with different price indexes. Types of volume indexes concern with the use of a **base year** since a change in the base year usually affects the rates of volume growth. Finally, the methods of obtaining volume of GDP by using those price indexes are discussed. As in other chapters in the present handbook, the presentation merely provides an introduction so that readers can have a general idea about the deflation procedures. Price indexes that reflect changes in quality and the appearance of new products are assumed to be given.

B. TYPES OF PRICE INDEXES

13.4.   A unit price index is an index created by dividing the price of an individual good or service in a given year by the price of the same item of a year used for comparison and then multiplying the result by 100 (see table T13.1 for an example). To create a price index of an individual good and service, statistical agencies collect the unit price of that product over time.

13.5.   Unit price indexes are the basic information that is used to derive more aggregate price indexes using a certain weighting scheme. For example, the aggregate consumer price index (CPI) is the sum of the consumer price indexes of detailed goods and servic_s consumed by households and weighted by the shares of each product in the basket of consumer goods and services (see table T13.2 for an example). Even a simple price index, such as for television sets, is an aggregate index. It has to reflect price changes of a class of products of different sizes, specifications and qualities that are changing over time. Different types of volume indexes, as discussed below, reflect the changes in the weight of each component in a basket of goods and services.

13.6.   The following price indexes at a very detailed level are the norms in statistical works:

   a) **Producer price indexes (PPIs)**: the price collected for a product included in PPIs is the revenue received by its producer. Sales and excise taxes are not included in the price because they do not represent revenue to the producer. Thus, PPIs are in fact indexes of **basic prices** in SNA terminology. PPIs cover both goods and services. In some countries, PPIs are called wholesale price indexes;

---

[10] The term "volume measure" is used for an aggregate without quantity and prices, such as value added or GDP, as opposed to a single product with measurable quantity and price.

b) **Consumer price indexes (CPI)**: the price reflects the actual payments by households. It is the SNA purchasers' price, and may also include imputed expense, such as for owner-occupied housing. In many countries, only transactions in urban areas are considered in the calculation of CPIs, which may not be representative of price changes in rural areas;

c) **Import and export price indexes**: price indexes measure the change over time in <u>transaction prices</u> (the market sale price) of goods and services exported from or imported into a country. Those prices are measured at c.i.f., including duties and freight and insurance costs. Export prices are measured at f.o.b. excluding duties and freight and insurance costs.

13.7.   In principle, separate price indexes of intermediate goods and gross capital formation at purchasers' prices can also be collected but are in fact rarely collected because of cost and also because the volume measurement of GDP can be computed by using PPIs instead.

13.8.   Other price indexes frequently collected are **labour cost indexes** for compensation of employees, where the unit is labour hour by type of occupation and industry.

13.9   **Price index of output measured at production costs** is an aggregate index, calculated by national accountants as the sum of weighted price indexes of all items in the production costs. The weights are the share of cost of each item in the total production cost the calculation is similar to the example given in table T13.2).

TABLE T13.1. UNIT PRICE INDEX: AN EXAMPLE

Year	Price of a ton of rice	Price index (1990=100)
1990	$300 US	100.0 [=(300/300)^{a}100]
2000	$200 US	66.7 [=(200/300)^{a}100]

TABLE T13.2. CONSUMER PRICE INDEX: AN EXAMPLE

Household consumption	Share of total consumption in the base year	Product price index for 2000 (1990=100)^a	Weighted price index for 2000 (1990=100)
	(1)	(2)	(1)x(2)/100
Food	30	66.7	20.01
Other goods and services	70	120.0	84.0
Total or CPI (aggregate index)	100		104.01

^{a}These indexes are detailed CPI for products.

C. TYPES OF VOLUME INDEXES

13.10.   Types of volume indexes are different methods of deriving a volume index for a group of various products whose price changes over time are different. The main difference in those methods is in the selection of the base year. **A base year** is the year for which price data at the most detailed level are collected and serve as benchmark data to weight different quantities to obtain one single volume index. The change of a base year affects real rate of growth, as will be explained below. **A reference year** is simply any given year selected so that a series of values with different base years can be compared. A change in the reference year should not change rates of growth.

13.11.   There are three types of volume indexes:

a) The Laspeyres volume index;
b) The Paasche volume index;
c) The Fisher volume index.

Laspeyres volume index

13.12. The Laspeyres volume index uses prices of a given base year (year 0) as fixed weights.

13.13. Quantities of the current year (q_t) are multiplied by prices of the base year (p_0) to obtain volume at base year prices. A volume index is created when volume of the current year at a base year prices is divided by volume of the base year. The quantity (**q**) in the formula below is used either for output or, in the case of national accounts, the basket of goods and services in final consumption expenditure, gross capital formation, exports and imports. Thus:

$$L_{qt}(p_0) = \Sigma p_0 q_t / \Sigma p_0 q_0$$

13.14. Using the weights of the base year ignores substitution effects and tends to give a higher rate of volume growth in years close to current year.

13.15. Until recently, the Laspeyres volume index was the most widely used index in national accounts.

Paasche volume index

13.16. Paasche volume index uses prices of a current year (p_t) as the base year fixed weights.

13.17. Quantities of two different years are multiplied by prices of the current year to obtain volume at the current year. A volume index is created when volume of the current year is divided by volume of the reference year (year 0). Thus:

$$P_{qt}(p_t) = \Sigma p_t q_t / \Sigma p_t q_0$$

13.18. The Paasche volume index tends to give a lower rate of growth at the years closer to the current year.

13.19. Until recently, the Paasche volume index was not used in national accounts.

Fisher volume index

13.20. The Fisher volume index is the geometric mean of the Laspeyres and Paasche indexes. Thus:

$$F_{qt} = (L_{qt})^{1/2} * (P_{qt})^{1/2}$$

13.21. It is called the ideal index, since the change of the base year would not affect rates of growth and the product of the price index and the volume index reflects the same change in current values.

13.22. The 1993 SNA recommends the use of the chain Fisher volume index, i.e., the Fisher index with annual base year change, even though the total volume is not equal to the sum of the components at constant prices when they are derived by the Fisher index. The main reason is that it leads to better estimates of recent growth rates.

13.23. With annual change of the base year, changes in prices and volumes of the two non-consecutive time periods are the product of the indexes, whether Laspeyres or Fisher, of the intervening years: hence the name chain index.

Volume index by type of volume indexes: an example

13.24. Data for the example is given for two years in table T13.3. .

Table T13.3. Data at current prices

	Year 0			Year 1		
	Quantity	Price	Value	Quantity	Price	Value
High-tech goods	15	3	45	30	4	120
Non-high-tech goods	5	4	20	30	1.8	54
Total			65			174

13.25. Using the data in table T13.3 and the formulas given above, the three types of volume indexes are derived and shown in table T13.4. The derivation is not shown here but will be used as an exercise at the end of the chapter.

Table T13.4. Types of volume indexes

	Year 0,0	Year 0,1
Laspeyres	100	323.08
Paasche	100	252.17
Fisher	100	285.43

13.26. Table T13.5 shows the data of year 1 valued at the price of year 0. By using the Fisher volume index in table T13.4 to extrapolate the total value of the year 1 at the price of year 0, the total value (65x285.43/100=185) is not the same as the sum of the components (90+120=210). By using the Laspeyres volume index to extrapolate, the total value of year 1 at the price of year 0 is, however, the same as the sum of the components (210). The Laspeyres volume index was widely used in the past; however, its deficiency is that it relies on prices of a past year as fixed weights for calculating volume index. Thus, it does not reflect the substitution of relatively cheaper products for relatively more expensive products, especially if the base year is far away from the current year. The Fisher index relies on the average structure and thus captures more of the substitution effects. In addition, the SNA recommends a change of base year annually to take care of substitution effect. With the chain index or the Fisher index, the rate of volume growth tends to be lower than the rate obtained by the Laspeyres index.

Table T13.5. Loss of additivity in using Fisher indexes at the price of year 0

	Year 0			Year 1 at year-0 prices		
	Quantity	Price	Value	Quantity	Price	Value
High-tech goods	15	3	45	30	3	90
Non-high-tech goods	5	4	20	30	4	120
Total at prices of year 0			65			210
Total at prices of year 0 using Laspeyres index (=65*3.2308)						210
Total at prices of year 0 using Fisher index (=65*2.8543)						185

Chain index, base year and reference year: an example

13.27.   The example in table T13.6 shows the use of the chain index and the difference between the base year and the reference year.

13.28.   From the data in row 2 of table T13.6, in which the base year (either a Fisher or Laspeyres index) is annually changed, it is possible to calculate the volume index of T_5 relative to T_0 by chaining the indexes together, as follows:

$$1.02 \times 1.03 \times 1.01 \times 1.04 \times 0.99 = 1.093$$

13.29.   Since the base year changes annually, it is possible to use any year as **a reference year** so that a series of comparable values can be created. For instance, line 2 shows the value of GDP using T_3 as the reference year. GDP at T_4 is obtained by multiplying GDP at T_3 by the volume index of T_4 shown above and dividing the result by 100. GDP at other years after T_4 is calculated in the same way by multiplying the volume index of the year with GDP of the previous year. GDP at the years before T_3 is calculated by dividing GDP of the previous year by the volume index of the year and then multiplying the result by 100.

Table T13.6. Difference between base year and reference year

	T_1	T_2	T_3	T_4	T_5
Volume index (previous year =100)	102	103	101	104	99
GDP in current prices of the base year			450.0		
GDP in T_0 prices	432.6	445.5	450.0	468.0	463.3

D. METHODS OF OBTAINING VOLUME OF GDP

General principles

13.30.   GDP at constant prices can be measured by measuring at constant prices the final uses of GDP, which consists of final consumption expenditure, gross capital formation and exports less imports. The final uses are deflated with their respective price indexes. That measurement is based on the final expenditure approach to GDP.

13.31. GDP at constant prices (volume measure) can also be measured by using the double deflation method, i.e., by deflating output and intermediate consumption with their respective price indexes for each industry and then obtaining value added by industry at constant prices as the difference. Since there are price indexes for industry output, products produced by each industry are deflated by PPIs and summed up to obtain industry output at constant prices. GDP at constant prices is the sum of value added by industry at constant prices plus deflated taxes less subsidies on products. Taxes or subsidies at constant prices may be derived by taxes/product or subsidies/product ratios of the base year if tax rates do not change. That measurement is based on the production approach to GDP.

13.32. The best approach is to combine the deflation of final uses and the double deflation of value added through the use of the supply and use tables of a base year in order to avoid a discrepancy in the volume of GDP by the two separate procedures. The general outline of the double deflation approach is shown in tables T13.7 to T13.9. To become familiar with that method, readers should consult the *Handbook of Input-Output Table Compilation and Analysis* (United Nations publication, Sales No. E.99.XVII.9), chap.XI.

Specific comprehensive methods

13.33. There are two ways to implement the deflation method using supply and use tables. In a full-fledged application of the double deflation method, supply and use tables for both the current and base years must be available. However, if only final expenditures, exports, imports, industry outputs and total intermediate consumption by industries are available, short cuts are to be used. Short cuts use either the intermediate consumption matrix and the domestic supply matrix of the base year supply and use tables as weights in the derivation of implicit price indexes for intermediate consumption by industries, or the supply and use tables updated for the current year using the RAS method (for the RAS method, see *Handbook of Input-Output Tables Compilation and Analysis, op.cit., chap IX*). Supply and use tables derived by the RAS method are preferable to the simple use of base-year information as weights.

The first method

13.34. The first method is described in table T13.7. It requires producer price indexes (PPIs) for outputs of industry, purchasers' price indexes for intermediate consumption, household final consumption (CPI), government final consumption, gross capital formation, and price indexes for exports and imports. The method in general produces statistical discrepancy between GDP by production approach and GDP by final expenditure approach because there is always inconsistency among the various price indexes, even if the supply and use tables at current prices are fully balanced. Another drawback is that price indexes for intermediate consumption are not normally collected. An approximation technique must therefore be applied.

TABLE T13.7. DEFLATION OF GDP AND FINAL USES: FIRST METHOD, VERSION 1

SUPPLY TABLE

	Industries A, B, C...
Industry output Product A Product B Product C...	• Products produced by industries are measured at basic prices and individually deflated by PPIs, the sum of which is industry output at constant prices

USE TABLE

	INTERMEDIATE CONSUMPTION	FINAL USES
Products used Product A Product B Product C ...	• Measured at purchasers' prices • Intermediate consumption by type of products is deflated by *price indexes for goods and services used for intermediate consumption*	• Measured at purchasers' prices • Gross capital formation (GCF) is deflated *by price indexes for goods and services used as GCF* • Final consumption is deflated by CPIs • Final consumption of government and NPISHs is deflated by production costs • Exports are deflated by export price indexes • Imports are deflated by imported price indexes
Value added	• Value added is derived as the difference between industry output and intermediate consumption	
Industry output	• Industry output at basic, constant prices is obtained from the supply table above	

13.35. Price indexes for intermediate consumption can be implicitly approximated in the following ways (see table T13.8):

a) Deflate the supply table to arrive at the total constant value of supply of products at purchases prices. To do that, outputs are deflated by PPIs, imports are deflated by import price indexes, and trade and transport margins at constant prices are derived by the ratios of trade margin over the value of product used (domestic product plus import) of the base year. The use of base-year trade margin ratios is based on the assumption that real trade mark-up does not change. In principle, deflators can be collected for trade mark-up, but that is rarely done since it is costly to do so. If products produced by industries are not available, the product mixes of the base-year supply table can be used to approximate outputs of products;

b) Equate the constant values of supply to the constant value of uses in the use table;

c) Deflate household final consumption by CPIs, government final consumption also by CPIs if price indexes are not available, gross capital formation by its price indexes of gross and exports by export price indexes;

d) Derive the implicit constant value of intermediate consumption by products by deducting components of final uses in constant prices from the total uses in constant prices. Derive implicit price indexes of intermediate consumption by products;

e) Use the implicit price indexes of intermediate consumption by products to derive the implicit price indexes of intermediate consumption by industries. The weights used in deriving those latter price indexes are either the intermediate consumption of the base-year use table or that of the current use table that can be derived by the RAS method (for the RAS method, see *Handbook of Input-Output Tables Compilation and Analysis, op.cit., chap. IX*);

f) Use the deflated industry outputs in the supply table and deduct intermediate consumption by industries from them to derive value added at constant prices;

g) Taxes or subsidies at constant prices are derived by taxes/product or subsidies/product ratios of the base year. The use of base-year ratios is based on the assumption that tax or subsidies rates do not change. If tax/subsidies rates change, they should be used to create their own deflators.

TABLE T13.8. DEFLATION OF GDP AND FINAL USES: FIRST METHOD, VERSION 2

The supply table at current prices of the current year

	Industry 1	Ind. 2	Ind. 3	Total domestic at basic prices	Imports c.i.f	Trade and transport Margins	Taxes less subsidies on products	Total supply at purchasers' prices
Product 1	177	35			18	37	13	
Product 2	12	84			9	30	7	
Product 3			70		0	-67	0	
Industry output	189	119	70					

The use table at current purchasers prices of the current year

	Industry 1	Ind. 2	Ind. 3	Intermediate consumption by industry	Exports	Final Expenditure	Total uses at purchasers' prices
Product 1					33	161	
Product 2		Data on intermediate consumption may not be available			12	60	
Product 3						3	
Value added							
Industry output	189	119	70				

The second method

13.36. The second method is presented in table T13.9. It requires only PPIs and import price indexes. In order to utilize only those price indexes, elements in the use table and final uses measured at purchasers' prices must be separated into three separate components: basic values, taxes, and subsidies on products and trade margins. Intermediate consumption, final consumption and gross capital formation at basic prices are deflated by PPIs. Imports are deflated by import price indexes. Taxes or subsidies and trade margins at constant prices are derived by taxes/product or subsidies/product ratios and trade margin/product ratios of the base year, as discussed in method one.

13.37. In both methods, since there are no price indexes for industry output, products produced by each industry must be deflated by PPIs of relevant products and the results summed up to obtain industry output at constant prices (see the supply table where products produced by each industry are recorded). In other words, the price indexes of industry outputs are implicitly derived by dividing industry outputs at current prices by industry outputs at constant prices.

13.38. It is not possible to derive the volume of GDP by deflating components of value added since operating surplus, a component of value added, is calculated as a residual and therefore has no price index.

TABLE T13.9. DEFLATION OF GDP AND FINAL USES: SECOND METHOD

SUPPLY TABLE

	Industries A, B, C...
Industry output Product A Product B Product C ...	• Products produced by industries are measured at basic prices and individually deflated by PPIs, the sum of which is industry output at constant prices

USE TABLE

	INTERMEDIATE CONSUMPTION Measured at purchasers prices and subdivided into:	FINAL USES Measured at purchasers prices and subdivided into:
Products used Product A Product B Product C ...	1. Intermediate consumption at basic prices: deflated by PPIs 2. Taxes less subsidies on products used as intermediate consumption: deflated by using base-year ratios 3. Trade margins on products used as intermediate consumption: deflated by using base-year ratios	1. Final uses at basic prices: deflated by PPIs 2. Taxes less subsidies on produces used as final uses: deflated by using base-year ratios 3. Taxes less subsidies on produces used as final uses: deflated by using base-year ratios
Value added	• Value added is derived as the difference between industry output and intermediate consumption	
Industry output	• Industry output at basic, constant prices is obtained from the supply table above	

EXERCISE ON VOLUME INDEXES

Show step-by-step how the Laspeyres, Paasche and Fisher volume indexes are derived using the data at current prices given below. Show the price index for each commodity and then show the volume indexes for each commodity and aggregates using different types of indexes.

Data at current prices

	Year 0			Year 1		
	Quantity	Price	Value	Quantity	Price	Value
High-tech goods	15	3	45	30	4	120
Non-high-tech goods	5	4	20	30	1.8	54
Total			65			174

EXERCISE ON DOUBLE DEFLATION METHOD – SHORTCUT

The following information on an economy with only two industry producing two products will be used for the exercises:

- Shares of products at basic prices produced by each industry in the base year.
- Shares of production costs of each industry in terms of industry output (intermediate consumption are broken down into products in basic prices used in production, trade margins and taxes on products).
- It is assumed that trade margins are part of the output of industry 2.

Supply table of the base year

Industry \ Shares	Industry 1	Industry 2
Product 1	0.8	0
Product 2	0.2	1.0
Industry output	1.0	1.0

Production costs in the use table of the base year

Industry \ Shares	Industry 1	Industry 2
Product 1 in IC	0.30	0.20
Product 2 in IC	0.25	0.10
Trade margin on IC	0.10	0.05
Taxes on products on IC	0.02	0.00
Value added	0.33	0.65
Industry output	1.00	1.00

Given also the following information on the current year:

Price index of product 1: 105
Price index of product 2: 103
Output of industry 1: 220

Output of industry 2: 120

Calculate for the current year:

1. Price indexes for industry output (without information on the products at current prices produced by each industry, one has to assume that the output structure of the supply table at the base year remains the same in the current year).
2. Industry output at constant prices.
3. Intermediate consumption at constant prices.
4. Intermediate consumption at current prices.
5. Total value added at constant prices and current prices (it is not possible to derive GDP since the total taxes less subsidies on products is not given, except those on intermediate consumption).
6. Implicit price index for total value added.

SOLUTIONS

SOLUTIONS TO EXERCISE ON VOLUME INDEXES

Table 1: Laspeyres volume indexes

	Values at year-0 prices		Volume index
	Year 0	Year 1	Year 0 = 100
High-tech goods	45	90 [=120*100/133.3]	200
Non-high-tech goods	20	120 [=54*100/45]	600
Total	65	210	323.08

Table 2: Paasche volume indexes

	Values at year-1 prices		Volume index
	Year 0	Year 1	Year 0 = 100
High-tech goods	60 [=45*(133.3/100)]	120	200
Non-high-tech goods	9 [=20*(45/100)	54	600
Total	69	174	252.17

Fisher volume indexes = (Laspeyres index)$^{1/2}$ x (Paasche index)$^{1/2}$

- High-tech goods = $(200^{1/2}$ x $200^{1/2}) = 200$
- Non-high-tech goods = $(600^{1/2}$ x $600^{1/2}) = 600$
- Total = $(323.08^{1/2}$ x $252.17^{1/2}) = 285.43$

SOLUTION TO EXERCISE ON DOUBLE DEFLATION METHOD

1. Price indexes of the output of industry 1 and industry 2 of the current year are calculated by assuming that the structure of output of the base year remains the same:

- The price index of an industry output is the weighted price indexes of products produced by that industry. The weights are from the supply table of the base year.

   Table 1

	Price index of industry 1	Price index of industry 2
Product 1	84 (=0.8x105)	0
Product 2	20.6 (=0.2x103)	103 (=1x103)
Industry output	104.6	103

2. Industry output of the current year at constant prices:

   Industry 1: 220*100/1.046 = 210.32
   Industry 2: 120*100/1.03 = 116.50

3. Intermediate consumption of the current year at constant prices:

- The intermediate consumption at the base year price is calculated by using the intermediate consumption shares of the base year. Intermediate consumption at constant prices of each industry are equal to the product of the intermediate consumption shares of the base year and the corresponding industry output at the base year price (see table 2 below, for example, 0.3x210.32=63.1). Trade margins at constant prices are equal to the product of trade margin shares of the base year and the corresponding industry output at the base year price, (for example, 0.1x210.32=21.03). Taxes and subsidies at constant prices are similarly calculated. Value added at base year prices is the difference between output and intermediate consumption.

4. Intermediate consumption of the current year at current prices

- The intermediate consumption in current prices is calculated for products by inflating the values at the base year prices by the appropriate product price indexes, (for example, 63.1x105/100=66.25). Trade margin and taxes on products are calculated by applying the corresponding ratios in the base year to the industry output in current prices, (for example, 0.1x220=22). Value added at current prices is the difference between output and intermediate consumption.

Table 2

	At base year prices		At current prices	
	Industry 1	Industry 2	Industry 1	Industry 2
Product 1	63.10	23.30	66.25	24.47
Product 2	52.58	11.65	54.16	12
Trade margin	21.03	5.82	22	6
Taxes on products	4.21	0	4.4	0
Value added	69.41	75.73	73.19	77.53
Industry output	210.32	116.50	220	120

5. Total value added at constant and current prices:

> Total value added of the current year at the base year prices: 69.41 + 75.73 = 145.14
> Total value added of the current year at current prices: 73.19 + 77.53 = 150.72

6. Implicit price index:

> Implicit price index for total value added: (150.72/145.14)*100 = 103.8

PART III

DATA COLLECTION AND ESTIMATION
METHODS IN SNA

Chapter 14

Data collection, compilation and estimation methods in national accounts: a summary

A. OBJECTIVES

14.1   The compilation of national accounts relies on three approaches: the production approach, the income approach and the final expenditure approach (see paras. 2.14-2.16 above)). Each of those approaches requires a different set of data. The best practice is to combine all of them simultaneously in the framework of the supply and use tables, which was explained in chapter XIII above in relation to the methods of obtaining the volume of GDP. The main objective of that best practice is to avoid the discrepancies in the three values of GDP volume obtained by applying the three different methods separately. Thus, the compilation relies not only on data collected but also on aggregates, such as value added and GDP, obtained as residuals through the national accounts compilation process.

14.2.   In addition, the balancing technique applied in balancing supply and use tables would yield information on the elements concerning which statisticians do not have direct information or when it is too costly to collect information directly. For example, grain production may be produced by numerous households but also by a few large corporations. The total output of grain is normally measured by the total crop area and estimated yield per acre. The total output of grain by corporations must be obtained by direct survey, but the total output of grain by households can be obtained as a residual. The total output of grain is then balanced with change in inventories, the intermediate use of grain in animal farming, a few manufacturing industries, and imports and exports of grain in order to obtain the total household consumption of grain. Thus, it is not necessary to survey households on their production and final consumption of grains.

14.3.   The present chapter will provide a general review of how data are collected and the estimation techniques used in national accounts compilation.

B. DATA-COLLECTION METHODS

14.4.   Data for national accounts come from three main sources:

  a) Administrative records;
  b) Statistical methods: data obtained by extrapolating survey results on the basis of a benchmark census, a complete enumeration of the entire population;
  c) Estimation methods in the national accounts departments.

14.5.   Those different types of data are reviewed below.

C. DATA FROM ADMINISTRATIVE RECORDS

Types of records

14.6.   The following records are prepared and submitted to higher authority by mandates:

a) Government revenue and expenditure statistics (traditionally compiled by the ministry of finance on government budget);
b) Foreign trade statistics (i.e., exports and imports of goods through customs);
c) Money and banking statistics (traditionally compiled by the central bank);
d) Report on insurance companies by the insurance regulatory authority;
e) Tax records, with limited information on sales, cost of sales and income (processed by tax authority);
f) Business accounts of publicly traded corporations submitted to the stock exchange regulation commission.

14.7.   The following records are prepared for internal uses by corporations:

a) Business accounts of corporations that include the income statement, the change in the financial position or cash-flow statement, and the balance sheet;
b) Market analyses by producers associations.

National accounts data in administrative records

14.8.   Administrative records can provide information on production accounts and final uses of the government sector (not only for general government but also for non-market services produced by the government), the financial corporations sector and the non-financial corporations sector.

14.9.   Government revenue and expenditure statistics, money and banking statistics and the financial information of insurance companies can provide information on transactions of property income and current transfers between various sectors of the economy, which is particularly useful for the compilation of the household sector.

14.10.   Taking advantage of administrative records in the compilation of national accounts depends on the agency responsible for compiling national accounts working closely with the agencies that are responsible for those records to specify the details that are necessary for national accounts; the ability to utilize those records; and the speed with which the records are made available.

Quality evaluation

14.11. For administrative records:

a) Coverage and reliability are high;
b) Timeliness is low since it takes time to process reports;
c) Processing cost can be high.

Correction measures to improve timeliness

14.12.   To speed up data availability of administrative records, a sampling of tax records may be utilized; the use of budgeted government revenues and expenditures, may be corrected for implementing indicators (based on past experience or current assessments).

14.13.   Revision of administrative records is needed when complete and/or audited data are made available.

D. DATA COLLECTED BY STATISTICAL METHODS

14.14.   A wide range of statistics are collected by government (national statistical offices) for purposes other than national accounts by censuses and surveys.

14.15.   A census of all statistical units in a given population is carried out every five or 10 years. Every year or quarter, a sample is taken to estimate population data. The process of data collection by census and surveys is shown in figure F14.1. The most important requirement for a sample survey to be reliable is that the register of statistical units (sometimes called the frame) is up to date.

CENSUS

Definition

14.16.   A census is a complete enumeration of an entire population of statistical units in a field of interest. For example, the population census canvases every household in a country to count the number of permanent residents and other characteristics, or a census of manufacturing may canvas all establishments engaging in manufacturing activities. The census of population (and households) is commonly carried out every 10 years. The censuses of agriculture, fishery, forestry, construction, manufacturing, trade and other services are commonly carried out every five years. Similarly, a consumer income and expenditure survey is carried out every five years.

14.17.   Data from the censuses serve as the base-year or benchmark data.

Requirement

14.18.   A complete and up-to-date register of all statistical units in the field of inquiry is required.

Advantages

14.19.   A census provides the most reliable statistics if done professionally and with integrity.

Disadvantages

14.20.   It is very costly to enumerate and to process data by means of a census. Timeliness is not high: data is available for use only many months, even years after it is collected. A census is normally carried every five or 10 years.

FIGURE F14.1. PROCESS OF DATA COLLECTION BY CENSUS AND SURVEYS

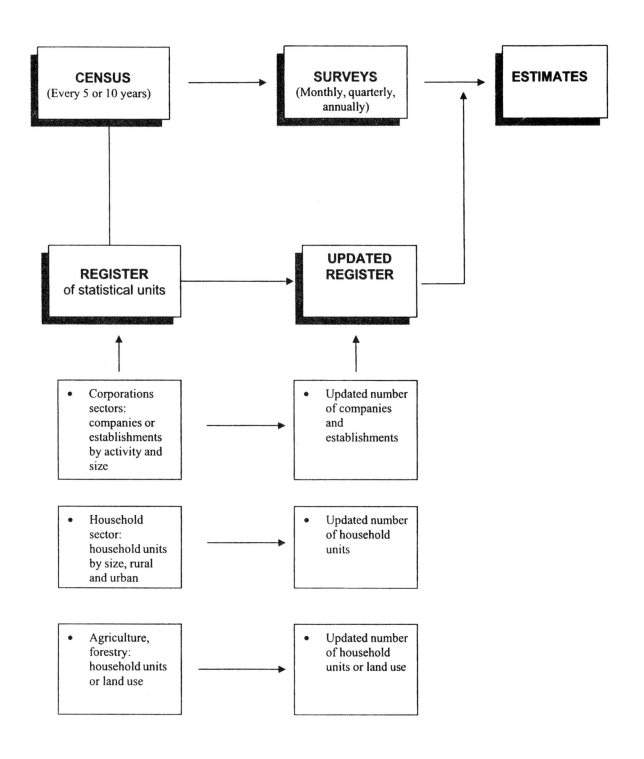

SURVEYS

Definition

14.21.   Surveys are based on a scientifically selected random sample from a population. Data for the population is obtained by blowing up the sample data by extrapolating the sample size to the population size.

Advantages

14.22.   Surveys provide more up-to-date statistics, which are reliable, if scientifically designed and professionally implemented, and are less costly than a census. Sampling errors can also be obtained. Surveys are normally carried out weekly, monthly, quarterly or annually.

Disadvantages

14.23.   Timeliness requires prompt data processing, thus less information may be gathered.

E. ESTIMATION METHODS IN SNA

14.24.   There are three methods of estimation in national accounts for data that are not available in administrative records, censuses or surveys:

a)   Balancing item method;
b)   Commodity flow method;
c)   Benchmark ratio method.

Balancing items

14.25.   As a system of identities, data for the national accounts on many important aggregates are obtained as balancing items. For example, value added is defined as a balancing item, i.e., output less intermediate consumption.

14.26.   The reliability of balancing items depends on the reliability of the basic information, which in the case above consist of output and intermediate consumption.

Commodity flow method

14.27.   Commodity flow method is based on the exploitation of the equality of supply and use of a commodity in the economy, i.e., output + import = final consumption + gross fixed capital formation + change in inventories + exports.

14.28.   Commodity flow method is widely used to obtain gross capital formation. For instance, machinery, a capital good, is supplied by domestic production (output obtained through surveys) and import (obtained by administrative records). Final consumption of that commodity by definition is zero. Given change in inventories (obtained through surveys) and exports (by administrative records), the good used as gross fixed capital formation can be obtained.

14.29.   If there are independent estimates of all the components, the commodity flow method is also used to balance supply and use of commodities in an economy.

Benchmark ratio method

14.30. Constant ratios of the most recent benchmark year, for instance value added/output ratios, are regularly used to extrapolate value added of the current period given output (obtained by survey). Quarterly national accounts rely even more heavily on the benchmark ratio method. For example, the quantity of electricity used may be used to extrapolate output and value added of the electricity activity, or retail trade data may be used to extrapolate household final consumption by product.

14.31. The advantage of this technique is that the use of ratios requires surveying only output, which is easier to obtain than intermediate consumption.

14.32. The drawback of this method is that it gives the impression that value added/output ratios are not volatile since it is assumed that technical change is slow, whereas of course such ratios are certainly not constant.

14.33. Value added of corporations, which may be directly obtained, can be used as total controls. However, it is not possible to get value added for the household sector directly since households do not keep business accounts, nor for the establishments sector for which only cost of production can be accounted for.

14.34. A simple way of estimating value added of the industries that produce commodities with highly fluctuating prices is as follows:

   a) Deflate output by its price index and then use the benchmark ratio to calculate value added at constant price;
   b) Estimate intermediate consumption at constant price and inflate it to current price by a composite price index of intermediate consumption;
   c) Estimate value added at current price by the difference between output and intermediate consumption at current price.

Evaluation of estimation methods

14.35. The production approach relies on all three types of data sources. Estimates based on surveys with updated benchmark ratios are more reliable than those based only on benchmark ratios of a distant year.

14.36. The income approach relies on surveys or administrative records but is applicable to corporations only. This approach is used less frequently than the production approach and the final expenditure approach.

14.37. The final expenditure approach relies mainly on surveys and administrative records:

   a) Data on final consumption and gross capital formation of government are obtained from government bookkeeping;
   b) Data on exports and imports of goods are obtained from customs, data on exports and imports of services from banking statistics and surveys;
   c) Data for gross capital formation for non-government sectors are obtained from direct surveys of capital formation or applying the commodity flow approach to data obtained by surveys and administrative records;

d) Data on final consumption of households are extrapolated from benchmark data, using retail trade surveys and household budget surveys. Without retail trade surveys, household consumption may have to be estimated as balancing items or residuals, a less reliable approach.

14.38. For GDP at constant prices:

a) The final expenditure approach provides the easiest way of obtaining GDP at constant prices;

b) The production approach has to rely on double deflation method, (i.e., deflating both output and intermediate consumption and then taking the difference between them to derive value added in constant prices). Since intermediate consumption contains numerous different goods and services for different industries, it is therefore not easy to apply this method quarterly or annually. In case data are not available, a single indicator method must be utilized. That indicator can be the consumer price index;

c) It is impossible to derive value added at constant prices by the income approach since it is not possible to deflate operating surplus.

ANNEX

EXPLANATION OF SNA SUPPLY AND USE TABLES
AND
INTEGRATED ACCOUNTING FRAMEWORK:
AN EXAMPLE

OBJECTIVES

A.1. The present annex aims to provide a detailed example of the full integrated accounting framwork of the SNA with a simplified example. The example is also contained in the Excel file SNA.xls in the diskette which is provided on the webpage of the United Nations Statistics Division http://unstats.un.org/unsd/sna1993/handbooks.asp.

A.2. The explanation also serves as instructions for using the SNA Excel compilation worksheets posted in the webpage mentioned above in the Excel file **SNA.zip**. The compilation worksheets are expected to provide developing countries with a simple and ready-to-use tool to compile sectoral accounts. Worksheets for the supply and use tables are not provided, since it is not possible to predict the appropriate industrial sectoring for a country. However, the supply and use tables can be easily extended from the supply and use tables supplied in the simplified example.

A.3. In the present example, the non-profit institutions serving households (NPISH) sector is aggregated to the general government sector for presentation purposes because both sectors produce mainly non-market goods and services and therefore SNA treats them similarly. In practice, the NPISH sector is either shown as a separate sector or aggregated to the household sector.

USE AND SUPPLY TABLES

SUPPLY TABLE

| | Output of industries at basic prices | | | | | Total economy | Imports c.i.f. (Total f.o.b.) | C.i.f./f.o.b. adjustment | Total product supply | Trade & transport margins | Taxes less subsidies on products | Total product supply at purchasers' prices |
| | Non-financial activities | | Financial activities | | Other non-market Government & NPISHs | | | | at basic prices | | | |
	Unincorporated enterprises	Corporate enterprises	Unincorporated enterprises	Corporate enterprises								
	(1)	(2)	(3)	(4)	(5)	(6)=(1)+..+(5)	(7)	(8)	(9)=(1)+..+(7)	(10)	(11)	(12)=(9)+..+(11)
1 Non-financial goods & services except margins[a]	44	239				283	22		305	60	15	380
2 Trade and transport services	10	53				63	3	-1	65	-60	3	8
3 Financial services			2	18		20	2	-1	21		2	23
4 Other non-market services					10	10	0		10			10
5 c.i.f./f.o.b. adjustment							-2	2	0			0
6 Direct purchases abroad by residents							3		3			3
7 Total supply at basic prices	54	292	2	18	10	376	28		404	0	20	424

USE TABLE

| | Intermediate consumption of industries | | | | | Total economy | Exports f.o.b. | Household final expenditure | Government & NPISHs | | Gross capital formation | Total use of products purchasers' prices |
| | Non-financial activities | | Financial activities | | Other non-market Government & NPISHs | | | | Individual final consumption | Collective final consumption | | |
	Unincorporated enterprises	Corporate enterprises	Unincorporated enterprises	Corporate enterprises								
	(1)	(2)	(3)	(4)	(5)	(6)=(1)+..+(5)	(7)	(8)	(9)	(10)	(11)	(12)
1 Non-financial goods & services except margins[a]	22	129	0	5	2	158	37	142	3		40	380
2 Trade and transport services	-	4	-	-	-	4	2	2				8
3 Financial services	2	12	0	1	2	17	1	5				23
4 Other non-market services		1				1		1	5	3		10
5 Direct purchases abroad by residents								3				3
6 Direct purchases at home by non-residents							1	-1				0
7 Total uses at purchasers' prices	24	146	0	6	4	180	41	152	8	3	40	424
8 Total gross value added/GDP						216						
9 Gross value added at basic prices	30	146	2	12	6	196						
10 Taxes less subsidies on products						20						
11 Industry output at basic prices/total	54	292	2	18	10	376						

[a] "Margins" refers to trade and transport margins.

INTEGRATED NATIONAL ACCOUNTING FRAMEWORK

	Non-financial corp. sector (1)		Financial corp. sector (2)		Government & NPISH sector (3)		Household sector (4)		Total economy (5)		Rest of the world sector (6)		Totals checking (7)	
	U	R	U	R	U	R	U	R	U	R	U	R	U	R
PRODUCTION ACCOUNTS														
1 Imports f.o.b.												28		28
2 Exports f.o.b.											41			
3 External balance of goods & services											*-13*			
4 Output at basic prices		292		18		10		56		376				
5 Intermediate consumption	146		6		4		24		180					
6 **Gross value added at basic prices**	*146*		*12*		*6*		*32*		*196*					
7 Taxes less subsidies on products									20				20	20
8 **GDP**									216					
GENERATION OF INCOME ACCOUNTS														
9 Gross value added at basic prices		146		12		6		32		196				
10 Compensation of employees	120		7		6		0		133				133	133
11 Wages and salaries	110		6		5		0		121				121	121
12 Employers social contributions	10		1		1		0		12				12	12
13 Other taxes on production	2		0		0		1		3				3	3
14 Taxes less subsidies on products														
15 **Gross operating surplus**	*24*		*5*		*0*				*29*					
16 **Gross mixed income**							*31*		*31*					
ALLOCATION OF PRIMARY INCOME														
17 External balance of goods & services												-13		
18 Gross operating surplus		24		5		0				29				
19 Gross mixed income								31		31				
20 Compensation of employees								131		131	3	5	136	136
21 Wages and salaries								119		119	3	5	124	124
22 Employers social contributions								12		12			12	12
23 Other taxes on production						3				3			3	3
24 Taxes less subsidies on products						20				20			20	20
25 Property income	14	11	10	8	4	4	2	10	30	33	3	0	33	33
26 **Balance of primary income/Gross national income**	*21*		*3*		*23*		*170*		*217*					
SECONDARY DISTRIBUTION OF INCOME														
27 Balance of primary income/gross national income		21		3		23		170		217				
28 Current taxes on income	8		1			59	50		59	59			59	59
29 Social contributions				30		10	40		40	40			40	40
30 Social benefits other than in kind	1		40		60			101	101	101			101	101
31 Other current transfers			9	20	3		20	21	32	41	10	1	42	42
32 **Gross disposable income**	*12*		*3*		*29*		*182*		*226*					

	Non-financial corp. sector (1) U	(1) R	Financial corp. sector (2) U	(2) R	Government & NPISH sector (3) U	(3) R	Household sector (4) U	(4) R	Total economy (5) U	(5) R	Rest of the world sector (6) U	(6) R	Totals checking (7) U	(7) R
REDISTRIBUTION OF INCOME IN KIND														
33 Gross disposable income		12		3		29		182		226				
34 Social transfers in kind					8			8	8	8			8	8
35 Social benefits in kind					3			3	3	3			3	3
36 Transfers of individual goods & services					5			5	5	5			5	5
37 Adjusted gross disposable income	12		3		21		190		226					
USES OF DISPOSABLE INCOME														
38 Gross disposable income		12		3		29		182		226				
39 Final consumption expenditures					11		152		163					
40 Adjustment for change in net equity of			10					10	10	10				
41 households on pension funds														
42 Gross saving	12		-7		18		40		63					
43 Current external balance												-23		
44 Actual final consumption (adjusted)					3		160		163					
CAPITAL ACCOUNTS														
45 Gross saving		12		-7		18		40		63				
46 Current external balance												-23		
47 Gross capital formation	25		2		5		8		40					
48 Consumption of fixed capital	7		1		2		2		12					
49 Net capital formation	18		1		3		6		28					
50 Acquisition less disposal of non-produced assets	2		0		0		-2		0					
51 Capital transfers, receivable										2		2		2
52 Capital transfers, payable	-1								-1		-1		-2	
53 Net lending (+) / Net borrowing (-)	-16		-9		15		34		24		-24		0	
FINANCIAL ACCOUNTS														
54 Net lending (+) / Net borrowing (-)	-16		-9		15		34		24		-24		0	
55 Net acquisition of financial assets	10		29		27		44		110		-4		106	
56 Net incurrence of financial liabilities		26		38		12		10		86		20		106
57 Currency and deposits and the like	2		1	11	2		9		14	11	-1	2	13	13
58 Securities other shares	2	2	7	9	10	12	13		32	23	-2	7	30	30
59 Loans	1	11	18	7	12			5	31	23		8	31	31
60 Shares and other equity	4	2	2	2	4				10	4	-3	3	7	7
61 Insurance technical reserves				18			18		18	18			18	18
62 Net equity on household life insurance				6			6		6	6			6	6
63 Net equity on household pension funds				10			10		10	10			10	10
64 Prepayment of premiums				1			1		1	1			1	1
65 Reserves against outstanding claims				1			1		1	1			1	1
66 Other accounts receivable/payable	5	2	1	2			1	5	5	7	2		7	7

	Non-financial corp. sector (1)		Financial corp. sector (2)		Government & NPISH sector (3)		Household sector (4)		Total economy (5)		Rest of the world sector (6)		Totals checking (7)	
	U	R	U	R	U	R	U	R	U	R	U	R	U	R
BALANCE SHEETS														
OPENING BALANCE SHEETS														
67 Non-financial assets	720		50		165		196		1131			0		
68 Produced assets	420		30		65		96		611					
69 Non-produced assets	300		20		100		100		520					
70 Financial assets/liabilities	85	180	330	310	37	70	172	40	624	600	54	25	678	625
71 Opening net worth		625		70		132		328		1155		29		1184
CHANGE IN THE BALANCE SHEETS from														
CAPITAL AND FINANCIAL ACCOUNTS														
72 Non-financial assets	20		1		3		4		28			0		
73 Produced assets	18		1		3		6		28			0		
74 Non-produced assets	2		0		0		-2		0			0		
75 Financial assets/liabilities	10	26	29	38	27	12	44	10	110	86	-4	20	106	106
OTHER CHANGES IN VOLUME & REVALUATION														
76 Non-financial assets	65		3		12		20		100					
77 Produced assets	40		2		4		10		56					
78 Non-produced assets	25		1		8		10		44					
79 Financial assets/liabilities	2	4	10	10	0	4	15	0	27	18	4	0	31	18
Change in net worth		67		-5		26		73		161		-20		141
80 Gross saving		12		-7		18		40		63		-23		
81 Consumption of fixed capital		-7		-1		-2		-2		-12		0		
82 Capital transfers		-1		0		2		0		1		-1		
83 Other changes in volume and revaluation		63		3		8		35		109		4		
CLOSING BALANCE SHEETS														
84 Non-financial assets	805		54		180		220		1259			0		
85 Produced assets	478		33		72		112		695			0		
86 Non-produced assets	327		21		108		108		564			0		
87 Financial assets/liabilities	97	210	369	358	64	86	231	50	761	704	54	45	815	749
88 Closing net worth		692		65		158		401		1316		9		1325

A. EXPLANATION OF SNA SUPPLY AND USE TABLES AND INTERGRATED ACCOUNTING FRAMEWORK: A SIMPLIFIED EXAMPLE

A.4.   The example contained in the annex table above presents numerically the complete SNA in a simplified manner but still retains all the essential features of the system. The example is also included in Excel spreadsheets so that readers can examine the relationships of all economic transactions in the economy with each other and with transactions with the rest of the world. It is modeled on the examples given in the *System of National Accounts, the 1993* (1993 SNA). Besides reading the text of explanations, readers may also explore all the relationships in the formulas set out in the Excel worksheets provided on the United Nations Statistics Division webpage. The worksheets are similar to those developed by the United Nations Statistics Division for actual national accounts compilation. The example may be used as a training tool before the software developed by the Division is used for actual compilation.

A.5.   The explanations given here are for the purpose of guiding readers through the example only. To understand the principles of national accounting, the compilation of supply and use tables and input-output tables, and the use of business accounts to compile the institutional sectoral accounts, readers should consult the 1993 SNA, the *Handbook of Input-Output Table Compilation and Analysis,* (United Nations publication, Sales No. E.99. XVII.9) and *Links between Business Accounting and National Accounting* (United Nations publication, Sales, No. E.00.XVII.13).

1. SUPPLY AND USE TABLES

A.6.   The supply table and the use table are both shown in a very aggregated manner. In the activity columns, all economic activities conducted by each institutional sector are aggregated into one column. In actual compilation, each column here may contain numerous columns, each of which is identified by an industry classification code, which should be based on ISIC, Rev.3 [a]. The reason for so doing is to immediately show the value added generated by every institutional sector in the economy and then have it linked to the integrated accounting framework for pedagogical purposes. The rows are also highly aggregated, may be much more numerous and are identified by the commodity classification codes, which should be based on CPC [b].

A.7.   In supply and use of tables, the total supply of each product must equal its total use. It is easy to check, in column 12, that the row sums from row 1 to 4 in the supply table are equal to the corresponding row sums in the use table. Thus:

      total supply = domestic production + imports
      total use   = intermediate consumption by industries + exports + final consumption + gross capital formation

A.8.   The outputs of industries in the supply table are at basic prices, but the uses in the use table are at purchasers' prices. Because of that, in the supply table, the supply of product at purchasers' prices (column 12) are obtained by adding to the supply of product at basic prices (column 9) the trade and transport margins (column 10) and taxes less subsidies on products (column 11).

---

[a] *International Standard Industrial Classification of All Economic Activities, Revision 3* (United Nations publication, Sales No. E. 90.XVII.11).
[b] *Central Product Classification Version 1.0* (United Nations publication, Sales No. E. 98.XVII.5).

A.9.   The elements of imports in the supply table (column 7) must be measured including cost, insurance and freight (c.i.f.) to make them equivalent to basic prices, but the total value of imports must be valued free on board (f.o.b.) so as to arrive at the correct balance of trade (imports less exports). Thus, the column and row of c.i.f./f.o.b. adjustment are necessary. In order to avoid double counting, the adjustment row and column (row 5 and column 8) deduct insurance and freight services on imported goods since they are included in both the values of imported goods and the supply of services.

A.10.   As with other outputs, the output of transport services is shown in row 2 and column 6 of the supply table. However, row 2 of the use table shows only the trade and transport services at purchasers' prices, which are directly purchased by users because trade and transport margins on the goods consumed are already included as a part of the purchasers' prices of goods that are used. Thus, to balance the totals of row 2 of the supply and use tables, the total value of trade and transport margins is entered in row 2 and column 10 of the supply table as a negative value.

A.11.   Reading through column 1 and row 1 of both the supply and use tables helps explain how data are presented. The total supply at purchasers' prices of product 1 [c] in row 1 is 380; 44 is produced by activity 1 and 239 by activity 2 and 22 is imported, so the total supply at basic prices is 305. Adding in trade and transport margins (for circulation inside the economy) (60) and taxes less subsidies on products (15), one obtains the total supply of the first product at purchasers' prices (380). Column 1 in the supply table shows the outputs at basic prices produced by activity 1. It produces two products: the output of product 1 (44) and the output of product 2 (10). Column 1 in the use table shows the uses of goods and services in production of those outputs; 24 (=22 + 2 shown in row 7) is called intermediate consumption. The gross value added (30) is calculated as the difference between the industry output of industry 1 (54) and its intermediate consumption (24). The value added may be broken down into compensation of employees, other taxes on production, consumption of fixed capital and operating surplus. Gross operating surplus, together with mixed income, is calculated as a residual. In case of unincorporated enterprises, which combine expenditures of the enterprise and final consumption expenditure of their owners so that compensation of employees is not paid explicitly to the owner/worker, the residual will be called mixed income.

A.12.   GDP is equal to the total of value added at basic prices plus taxes less subsidies on production and imports. GDP = 196 + 20 = (30 + 146 + 2 + 12 + 6) + 20 = 216 (see use table, column 6, rows 8 to 10. Taxes less subsidies on products are obtained as the sum of column 11 in the supply table, and are also shown in the use table in column 6, row 10. Taxes and subsidies are not shown elsewhere in row 10 since producers pay for them only as part of their intermediate consumption.

A.13.   GDP also must equal the sum of exports, household final expenditure, government and NPISH final expenditures, gross capital formation *minus* imports. GDP = 41 + 152 + 8 + 3 + 40 − 28 = 216.

A.14.   The output, intermediate consumption and value added by institutional sectors shown in the supply and use tables of the integrated framework are derived from the table of cross-classification of output, intermediate consumption and value added by economic activity and institutional sector. The following is a simplified table (the cross- classification requires that each economic activity be identified with the institutional sector under which it operates):

---

[c] The outputs in the supply and use tables in the present example are shown in terms of types of enterprises in order to link them to those of the institutional sectors. However, they will normally be shown in terms of industries classified by ISIC. The description in the present example treats them as though they are industry output.

Cross-classification of output, intermediate consumption and value added by economic activity and institutional sectors

	Agriculture forestry, fishery, mining	Manufacturing utility construction	Trade, Transport Communication	Financial intermediation	Education, health, social and other Non-market services	Total economy
	(1)	(2)	(3)	(4)	(5)	(6)=(1)+..+(5)
OUTPUT at basic prices	33	179	64	20	80	376
Non-financial corporations sector	20	153	49		70	292
Financial corporations sector				18		18
Households sector/NPISH	13	26	15	2		56
General government sector					10	10
INTERMEDIATE CONSUMPTION at purchasers' prices	8	110	31	6	25	180
Non-financial corporations sector	6	93	26		21	146
Financial corporations sector				6		6
Households sector/NPISH	2	17	5			24
General government sector					4	4
GROSS VALUE ADDED at basic prices	25	69	33	14	55	196
Non-financial corporations sector	14	60	23		49	146
Financial corporations sector	0			12		12
Households sector/NPISH	11	9	10	2		32
General government sector					6	6

2. INTEGRATED NATIONAL ACCOUNTING FRAMEWORK

Rules of organization

A.15.   The Intergrated National Accounting Framework (INAF) is a sequence of T-accounts, unlike the supply and use tables, which is in a matrix form. In this T-account system, uses (or assets) are shown on the left and resources (or liabilities) are shown on the right. The difference between the sum of resources (R) and the sum of uses (U) in each accounts is called the balancing item. The balancing items in the example worksheet are in bold and shown on the left of the accounts. For example, the output of the non-financial sector is 292 (4,1R - which is row 4, column 1R), its intermediate consumption is 146 (5,1U) and gross value added at basic prices is the balancing item, 146 = 292 – 146 (6,1U).

A.16.   Moving from one account to another account, for example from *production accounts* to *generation of income accounts*, the balancing item of the previous account shown on the left (6,1U) is moved to the right as resources for the next account (9,1R).

A.17.   Transactions in the rest of the world accounts are recorded from the point of view of the rest of the world. Thus expenditures of the economy are recorded as receipts of the rest of the world and vice versa. For example, imports of the country (expenditures) are recorded as resources (receipts) of the rest of the world.

A.18.   For the total economy (columns 5U, 5R), its total uses are the sum of uses of all institutional sectors; its total resources are also similarly calculated. For example, 376 (4,5R) = 292 (4,1R) + 18 (4,2R) + 10 (4,3R) + 56 (4,4R).

A.19.   For error checking along the rows, whenever appropriate, the total uses of the total economy and the rest of the world must equal their total resources (see column 7). However, there is an exception to that rule when it is applied to the financial assets/liabilities in the balance sheets (rows 67-88). If one looks at row 70, columns 7, the total uses are not equal to the total resources, since one item, monetary gold and special drawing rights (SDRs) in assets, do not necessarily have the counterpart sectors that hold liabilities.

Production accounts

A.20.   Imports and exports are shown only in the rest of the world accounts. Imports of the country are recorded as resources and exports are recorded as uses.

A.21.   Imports, exports, output, intermediate consumption, taxes less subsidies on products are all obtained from the supply and use tables.

A.22.   GDP (216) is obtained by adding gross value added (196) to taxes less subsidies on product (20).

Generation of income accounts

A.23.   In these accounts, gross value added at basic prices is broken down into compensation of employees, other taxes and subsidies on productions. Gross operating surplus are calculated as residuals. No consumption of fixed capital is shown here, but if it is available it can be deducted from gross operating surplus to obtain (net) operating surplus.

A.24.   Gross mixed income, the balancing item in the household sector, is conceptually similar to gross operating surplus since it is calculated residually. This concept is used if it is not possible to distinguish between compensation of employees and operating surplus. The separation of gross operating surplus (15,5U) and gross mixed income (16,5U) in the example is mainly for the purpose of identification. Household or unincorporated enterprises may also pay out compensation to employees, so actual production accounts may have positive values for compensation of employees here.

Allocation of primary income accounts

A.25.   For checking the equality of the total uses and resources in each row of these accounts, the information from the *generation of income accounts* has to be used. The total uses of the economy, for each transaction in a row in the *generation of income accounts,* must be added to its uses by the rest of the world in the *allocation of primary income accounts* to make them equal to the total resources in the *allocation of primary income accounts.* For example, the total uses of compensation of employees in (20, 7U), which is 136, are equal to 133 (10,5U) + 3 (20,6U), which must equal the total resources shown in the allocation of income accounts (20,7R).

Redistribution of income in kind accounts

A.26. Social transfers in kind paid by the government and NPISH sector are also shown as the individual final consumption of that sector in the use table (column 9). Social benefits in kind (3) are the goods and services bought by the government and NPISH sector and then transferred to the household sector or bought by households and reimbursed by the government and NPISHs (column 9, row 1). Transfers of individual goods and services (5) are part of the non-market output of the industry producing government and NPISH services that benefit households less sales. The same goods and services bought by the government and NPISH sector are then transferred to the household sector in the use table (column 9, row 4).

A.27. Because of the existence of social transfers in kind, adjusted disposable incomes are obtained as balancing items. They are the actual disposable incomes of the institutional sectors. Those incomes must be compared to the actual final consumption (in row 44) to derive gross saving (row 45).

Uses of disposable income accounts

A.28. Gross disposable income in these accounts is moved *from the secondary distribution of income accounts,* not from *the redistribution of income in kind accounts.*

A.29. As already mentioned in paragraph 24, the same gross saving can also be obtained by deducting actual final consumption (row 44) from adjusted disposable income (row 37). Actual final consumption is obtained by deducting social transfers in kind (row 34) from the final consumption expenditures (row 39).

A.30. The adjustment for change in net equity of households on pension funds is recorded as transferred from pension funds in the financial corporations sector to the household sector. Here, transfers may be made from other sectors if they include pension funds. That adjustment should not affect the gross saving of the total economy.

A.31. The current external balance, the balancing item in the rest of the world sector (43,6U), is conceptually similar to gross saving of other domestic sectors although it is shown in a separate row. The balancing item is calculated as the external balance of goods and services (17,6R) + all other resources of the rest of the world − all other uses of the rest of the world, which is −13 + (5+1) − (3+3+10) = -23.

Capital accounts

A.32. For total checking, capital transfers receivable must be exhausted by capital transfers payable (see rows 51-52, column 7).

A.33. Net lending (+)/net borrowing (-) of the total economy and the rest of the world must be equal in absolute values, but with opposite signs.

Financial accounts

A.34. The balancing items in these accounts are presented at the top of the accounts instead of at the bottom. Items in row 54 are equal to the net acquisition of financial assets in row 55 *minus* the net incurrence of financial liabilities in row 56. The net acquisition is the sum of the net assets shown below. Similarly, the net incurrence is the sum of net liabilities shown below.

A.35. For error checking, not only must net lending/net borrowing for each institutional sector derived in the *financial accounts* equal that derived from *capital accounts, but also* the net acquisition must equal the net incurrence for the totals and for each individual transaction item..

Balance sheets

A.36. In the balance sheets, the closing balance sheets are equal to the opening balance sheets plus changes from the capital and financial accounts and changes due to other changes in volume and revaluation. Other changes in volume are due to disappearance or appearance of assets/liabilities that are not due to production, such as discovery, natural calamities, confiscation, reclassification etc. Since the revaluation of assets and liabilities is due to real holding gains/losses and/or effects of general price level, the latter is called neutral holding gains/losses.

A.37. Changes in the balance sheets from capital and financial accounts are shown here for pedagogical purposes; in the actual compilation framework, they can be obtained directly from the capital and financial accounts.

A.38. The net worth is obtained as the balancing item between the total of assets and the total of liabilities in a balance sheet. Change in the net worth can be calculated as the difference between the net worth of the closing balance sheet and that of the opening balance sheet. Change in the net worth can also be calculated as the sum of gross saving less consumption of fixed capital, plus net capital transfers and other changes in volume and revaluation (see rows 80-83).

A.39. The balance sheets shown in the example are not very detailed, particularly for financial assets/liabilities. In actual compilation, they should be at least as detailed as those shown in the financial accounts (rows 56-66). However, at the level of aggregation in our example, it is not easy to see the reason for the inequality of the total of financial assets and that of financial liabilities in the balance sheets (at the column of total checking). In fact, with more details, the total of each financial asset item must equal the total of its liabilities, except for monetary gold and SDRs. Transactions in existing monetary gold and SDRs in the financial accounts must have counterparts. However, when monetary gold or SDRs are created or withdrawn, they are recorded, unlike transactions in existing monetary gold, in the *other changes in volume accounts*, which makes the total of financial assets differ from that of financial liabilities. The difference is the value of monetary gold or SDRs, which does not have a liability counterpart.

A.40. Additions to the non-produced non-financial assets, such as the improvement or reclamation of land, are treated as part of production output and gross capital formation. In the balance sheets, they are then reclassified to non-produced assets. That reclassification, which is part of other change in volume, is not introduced in our example.

3. STRATEGIES FOR BALANCING INAF

A.41. To make easy the balancing of each transaction (i.e., the total use must equal the total resource in column 7), it is important to work with detailed information. For example, property income (line 25) can be broken down into interest from banks, interest on government bonds, interest on foreign loans, other interests; dividends, withdrawals from income of quasi-corporations, reinvested earnings on direct foreign investment; property income attributed to insurance policy holders; rents on land and sub-soil assets; and royalties on intangible non-produced assets, such as patented entities, leases and transferable contracts. Similarly, other current transfers may be broken down to net non-life insurance premiums, net life insurance premiums, current transfers within general government, immigrants' remittances, current transfers to NPISHs (if not much is known about current transfers to NPISHs, at least, its output less sales may be estimated to equal the current transfers they received when there are no other sources of income). Compilers should consult the 1993 SNA, the kind of data available in the country and break down the transactions in the compilation framework appropriately.

A.42.   Besides balancing each transaction, the full balancing of aggregates for the total economy is also important in the process of balancing. For instance:

a)   Gross disposable income = GDP + net factor income with the rest of the world + net current transfers with the rest of the world = 216 + (3 + 3 -5) + (10 − 1) = 226. This means that the value 226 can be obtained given GDP and the rest of the world accounts since transactions between resident sectors cancel each other out. Similarly, gross saving and net lending (+)/net borrowing (-) can be obtained given final consumption, gross capital formation and net capital transfers. Adjustment for change in net equity of households on pension funds (line 40) would not affect gross saving of the economy. That strategy also means that given reliable rest of the world accounts and production accounts, it is possible to obtain reliable estimates of gross disposable income, gross saving and net lending (+)/net borrowing (-) for the whole economy to be used as control totals;

b)   In the production accounts, estimates of outputs, total intermediate consumption and compensation of employees may be more reliable for the corporate financial and non-financial sectors and the government sector. The number of enterprises in those sectors are also much less numerous than those in the household sector (i.e. unincorporated enterprises). Thus, more efforts to improve data collection should be focused on those sectors;

c)   When discrepancy in net lending occurs, assuming that the rest of the world account is reliable, it is likely that the major estimates of the economy have problems. The following relationship has to be examined:

GDP = final consumption of household and NPISH sectors + final consumption of general government sectors + gross capital formation of the non-financial sector + gross capital of the financial sector + gross capital formation of the general government sectors + gross capital of the household and NPISH sectors + exports − imports.

In general, data for the household and NPISH sectors (either final consumption or gross capital formation) is the weakest. They must be re-examined carefully.

4. SECTORING THE ECONOMY

A.43.   SNA recommends breaking the economy down into at least five resident sectors: the non-financial corporate sector, the financial corporate sector, general government, NPISHs, and the household sector. However, for analytical purposes it may be important to break these sectors into more detailed sub-sectors: For example:

a)   The non-financial corporate sector may be broken down into oil and non-oil sectors if the economy relies heavily on income and taxes from oil exporting;
b)   The financial sector may be broken down into:
   i.   The central bank;
   ii. Deposit money corporations (commercial banks);

    iii. Other deposit money corporations (trustee savings banks, savings banks, loan associations, credit unisons, mortgage banks, building societies, post office savings banks etc.);

    iv. Other financial intermediaries except insurance corporations and pension funds (corporations financing investment, corporations involving financial leasing, hire purchase, consumer credit);

    v. Financial auxiliaries (securities, insurance and loan brokers, flotation corporations, corporations involving in arranging hedging instruments);

    vi. Insurance corporations and pension funds;

c) The government sector may be broken down into:

    i. Central government;

    ii. State government;

    iii. Local government;

    iv. Social security funds;

d) In addition, each institutional sector may be broken down further into public and private sub-sectors for the studying of their economic efficiency;

e) In our pre-programmed worksheets on SNA compilation, the following institutional classification is adopted:

    i. Non-financial sectors: public and private.

    ii. Financial sectors: central bank, depository banks (comprising SNA deposit money corporations, other depository corporations), non-bank (comprising other financial intermediaries except insurance and pension funds, and financial auxiliaries), individual life insurance, individual non-life insurance, social insurance and individual pension funds. Individual insurance consists only of insurance that is bought by individuals. Insurance and pension bought on the condition of employment (partly paid by employers) are classified into social insurances. In case it is not possible to distinguish individual and group insurances, one may classify them together. Social security funds operated and run by the government is classified in the government sectors.

    iii. General government sectors: central and local;

    iv. Household sector;

    v. NPISH sector.

B. SNA COMPILATION WORKSHEETS: A COMPILATION FRAMEWORK

General introduction

A.44.   The worksheets are posted at http://unstats.un.org/unsd/sna1993/handbooks.asp under Handbook, *National Accounts: A Practical Introduction*. Readers are advised to read the explanations of a simplified example contained in annex I for a better understanding of the compilation spreadsheets.. However, SNA COMPILATION does not include the supply and use tables: it is assumed that they are compiled elsewhere and the results transferred to SNA COMPILATION.

A.45.   SNA COMPILATION is a compilation framework in Excel developed by the United Nations Statistics Division. It includes 15 separate files:

➤ One central framework file, CENTRAL.XLS, which picks up information from individual institutional sector file and balance total use and total resource of each transaction and then provides statistical discrepancy (on the first column). Discrepancy = total resources – total uses.

➤ Two non-financial sector files, NFprivate.xls and NFpublic.xls, one for private corporations and one for public corporations.

➤ Seven financial sector files: Central Bank.xls for the central bank; Depository Bank.xls for depository banks and other deposit money corporations; NonBank.xls for other financial intermediaries except insurance corporations and pension funds, financial auxiliaries, such as securities, insurance and loan brokers, and hedging instrument arrangers; Life Insurance.xls for insurance corporations that issue private life insurance; NonLife Insurance.xls for non-life insurance corporations that issue private non-life insurance to cover risks, accidents, sickness, fire and deaths; Private Pension.xls for pension funds; Social Insurance.xls for all types of insurances that are compulsory either by law or by the conditions of employment or are encouraged by the intervention of employers; such as social security, life and non-life insurance partly paid by employers (see paras. 4.83-4.103 and annex IV of the 1993 SNA for definitions).

➤ Two government sector files, General Government, Central.xls for central government and General Government, Local.xls for local government (see paragraphs 4.104-4.131 of the 1993 SNA for definitions and sectoring).

➤ One household sector file: household.xls.

➤ One NPISH file: NPISH.xls.

➤ One rest of the world file: row.xls.

➤ Another file, MAIN.XLS, is also provided; it is just a convenient file so that users can go from CENTRAL file to institutional file and vice versa.

A.46.   All the files are stored in SNA.zip. To install the files, a folder with the name SNA COMPILATION (or any other name) must be created first in a hard disk, then SNA.zip is copied and unzipped into it. A click on any file will automatically open it.

A.47.   In the central framework, the totals of the non-financial sectors, financial sectors, government sectors, household and non-profit institutions serving households, and the total economy are automatically calculated.

A.48.   The system can be expanded to include more sectors by inserting two more columns for each additional sector in CENTRAL.XLS; for instance, deposit banks may be split into private and public sub-sectors. The same formulas for deposit banks can be copied into the new columns. However, it is important that the file name in the formulas in the new and old sectors be changed, and the financial subtotal in the central framework must also be modified to take into account the additional sector. In the system, structurally, the financial, non-financial, government, household and NPISH sectors are the same within the same kind of sectors but not the same across different kind of sectors.

A.49.   The system can be expanded to include more transactions (rows) but it is difficult to do so because in the CENTRAL.xls file, which picks up information from the individual institutional sector file, each data element in the institutional sector file is identified by fixed location of the row and column of the element. To modify, each element in the CENTRAL.XSL file must be changed.

Data entry into SNA COMPILATION

A.50.   An individual compiler can independently work with a sector file. After completing the data, the file is copied into the <u>SNA COMPILATION</u> folder.

A.51.   After the sector files are completed and copied into the system, the central framework file (CENTRAL) will take data from the sector files and automatically compile information for the total economy and the statistical discrepancies (SD), which are shown in the columns on the left side of the central framework. Non-zero in a line means that the total use and total resource of the transaction in the line is not equal. Discrepancy is shown in line 241, when net lending of the economy is not equal in absolute value but with opposite signs to net borrowing from the rest of the world (ROW) calculated for the capital account. Line 247 shows SD between the whole economy and ROW for the financial accounts. Capital accounts and financial accounts are compiled independently, but net lending/ borrowing compiled from either one of them must be the same. When they are not the same, SD will be non-zeros in line 483; similarly, SD in changes in net worth in the two accounts is shown in line 484.

A.52.   Data should be entered only in the lines and cells identified in black colour. Data should not be entered in lines or cells in green color since they contain formulas. In order to avoid erasing formulas mistakenly, a copy of all the original files should be kept.

A.53.   In the central framework file, <u>CENTRAL.XLS</u> data on taxes and subsidies on products are the only data that need to be entered. All other data are taken automatically from individual sector files.

A.54.   To balance the system, changes in data should be inputted in individual sector files. A printout of the central framework is also necessary in the balancing work.

A.55.   The <u>allocation of primary income</u> accounts, unlike SNA, is *not* subdivided into the <u>entrepreneurial income</u> (upper accounts) and <u>allocation of other primary income</u> accounts (lower accounts) because the entrepreneurial income account can be easily calculated from the allocation of primary income accounts, and to include it would require splitting the primary income account into two sub-accounts for which statistical discrepancies cannot be calculated.

A.56.   In the <u>use of adjusted disposable income</u> accounts of the household sector accounts file, actual individual consumption is automatically calculated as the sum of individual consumption expenditure and social transfers in kind. Social transfers in kind include individual government output net of sales, NPISH output net of sales, and government and NPISH social benefits in kind.

A.57.   In the balance sheets, data should be entered into <u>other changes in volume</u>, <u>revaluation</u> and <u>neutral holding gains</u> accounts and <u>opening balance sheets</u>. Data in <u>real holding gains</u> accounts, <u>changes in balance sheets</u> and <u>closing balance sheets</u> are automatically calculated.

كيفية الحصول على منشورات الأمم المتحدة

يمكن الحصول على منشورات الأمم المتحدة من المكتبات ودور التوزيع في جميع أنحاء العالم . استعلم عنها من المكتبة
التي تتعامل معها أو اكتب إلى : الأمم المتحدة ، قسم البيع في نيويورك أو في جنيف .

如何购取联合国出版物

联合国出版物在全世界各地的书店和经售处均有发售。请向书店询问或写信到纽约或日内瓦的
联合国销售组。

HOW TO OBTAIN UNITED NATIONS PUBLICATIONS

United Nations publications may be obtained from bookstores and distributors throughout the
world. Consult your bookstore or write to: United Nations, Sales Section, New York or Geneva.

COMMENT SE PROCURER LES PUBLICATIONS DES NATIONS UNIES

Les publications des Nations Unies sont en vente dans les librairies et les agences dépositaires
du monde entier. Informez-vous auprès de votre libraire ou adressez-vous à : Nations Unies,
Section des ventes, New York ou Genève.

КАК ПОЛУЧИТЬ ИЗДАНИЯ ОРГАНИЗАЦИИ ОБЪЕДИНЕННЫХ НАЦИЙ

Издания Организации Объединенных Наций можно купить в книжных магазинах
и агентствах во всех районах мира. Наводите справки об изданиях в вашем книжном
магазине или пишите по адресу: Организация Объединенных Наций, Секция по
продаже изданий, Нью-Йорк или Женева.

COMO CONSEGUIR PUBLICACIONES DE LAS NACIONES UNIDAS

Las publicaciones de las Naciones Unidas están en venta en librerías y casas distribuidoras en
todas partes del mundo. Consulte a su librero o diríjase a: Naciones Unidas, Sección de Ventas,
Nueva York o Ginebra.

Litho in United Nations, New York
02-76421—March 2004—2,450
ISBN 92-1-161469-4

United Nations publication
Sales No. E.04.XVII.4
ST/ESA/STAT/SER.F/85